Contents

. World Famous .

TRUE GHOST STORIES

Colin Wilson, Damon Wilson
and Rowan Wilson

MAGPIE
London

Magpie Books Ltd
7 Kensington Church Court
London W8 4SP

First published in the UK 1994

ISBN 1 85813 379 3

Typeset by Hewer Text Composition Services, Edinburgh
Printed in Finland by
Werner Söderström Oy

• chapter one •

THE INVASION OF THE SPIRIT PEOPLE

The "Exorcist" Poltergeist

The story of the haunted boy of Washington sounds like some absurd tale of medieval witchcraft; in fact, it is a true occurrence, and formed the basis of William Blatty's bestselling novel *The Exorcist*.

In January 1949, the Deen family, who lived in a suburb of Washington DC, began to wonder if they had a plague of rats; loud scratching noises came from the walls of the house and from the attic. But a company of rodent exterminators could find no trace of rats. The noises grew louder, until it was almost impossible to get a good night's sleep. Creaking sounds in the hallway sounded like cautious footsteps. Then the real "haunting" began. Dishes began to fly through the air, furniture moved of its own accord, a picture floated off the wall then floated back again, and fruit flew out of a bowl and smashed itself on the walls and floor.

By this time, the Deens realised they had a poltergeist. The word is German for "noisy ghost" – some of the earliest recorded cases occurred in Germany. Poltergeists seem to be the juvenile delinquents of the spirit world, and they delight in causing noise and confusion. The Washington poltergeist did more than that; within weeks, the whole family was on the point of nervous breakdown. But one thing was obvious: that the "spirit" centred its activities around their thirteen-year-old son, Douglass. The strange phenomena only occurred when he was in the room. And when he was out of the house, they stopped altogether.

Now the next stage began: Douglass's bed began to shake and tremble; it happened even when he was fast asleep. The distraught family asked the advice of their local minister, the Rev. Winston. He was inclined to be sceptical, but invited the boy to spend the night in his home; he set up a spare bed in his own bedroom. Douglass arrived at 9:20 on 17 February 1949, and at 10 o'clock he went off to bed. Within ten minutes, his bed was vibrating, and there were scratching noises from the wall. The minister hastily switched on the light, and saw that the boy was lying perfectly still, while his bed was shaking violently. He suggested that Douglass should sleep in a huge armchair, whose sheer size and weight should make it disturbance-proof. But as soon as the boy was tucked up in a blanket, the armchair began to move. First it rolled back against the wall, then it tilted until it shot the boy on to the floor. The minister was so curious that he tried sitting in the chair and making it tilt over; it proved to be impossible.

The boy finally had to sleep on a mattress on the floor. But even this slid about the room for the rest of the night, so that no one got much sleep. The next day the boy went into the Georgetown Hospital, a Catholic institution, for observation. Meanwhile, the minister gave a lecture to the Parapsychology Society, describing the amazing things he had witnessed.

When the hospital failed to solve Douglass's problem, they asked the help of the Jesuits. They decided that Douglass Deen was "possessed" by an "entity", and called upon the aid of a priest who specialised in exorcism, or the casting out of evil spirits. He spent several months fasting and repeating exorcism rituals over the boy, culminating in the words: "I command you, whoever you are, unclean spirit, that by our Lord Jesus Christ, you give me your name and the day of your exit . . ." For weeks this had no effect whatsoever; then Douglass began to shriek obscenities in a shrill voice, and to speak rapidly in Latin, a language he had never studied. It took until May 1949, but finally the "spirit" went away, and Douglass Deen became a normal teenager once more.

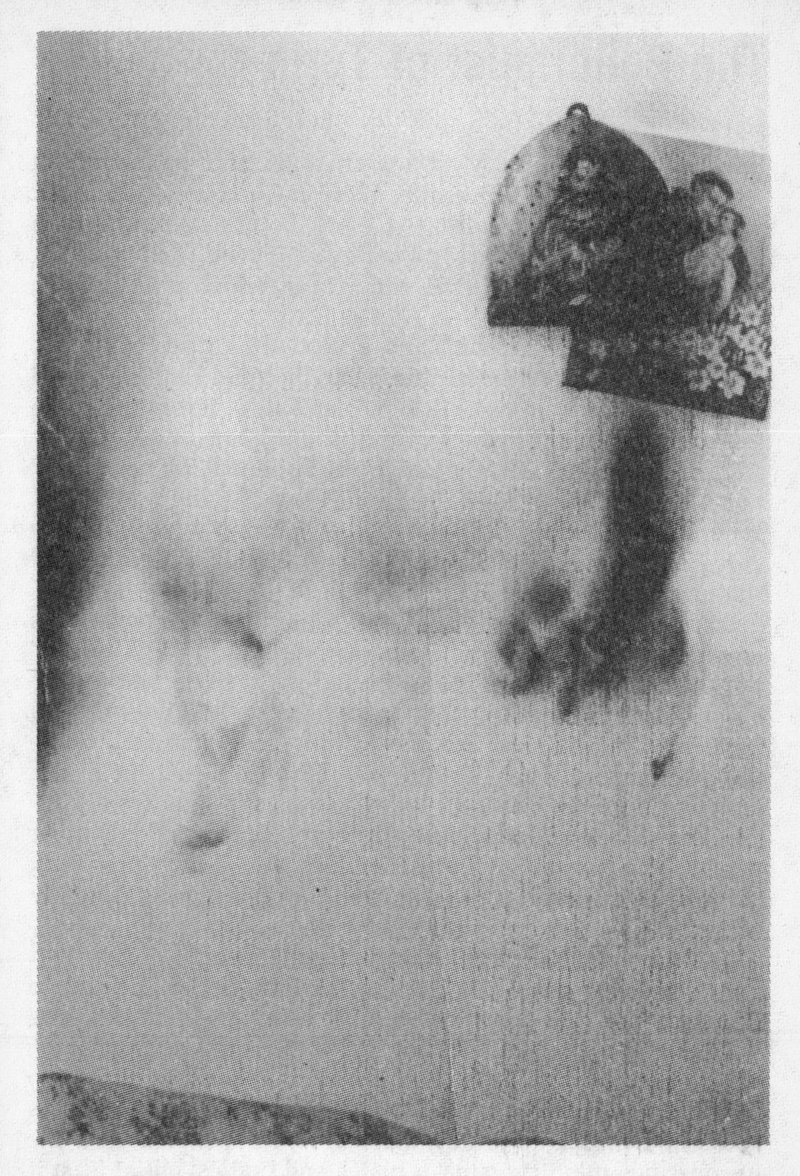

1972, this image of 'the Devil' appeared in Rome after an exorcism, according to a Roman Catholic Priest. He said the image resembling a malevolent goat seared on to a white plaster wall was accompanied by a series of savage blows on the wall which was suddenly enveloped in a sheet of flames, indicating that the Devil had left the young man being exerocised.

The Poltergeist of Turin

But *was* it an evil spirit? Most modern authorities on the subject would answer no. In November 1900, the famous psychologist – and sceptical materialist – Cesare Lombroso heard of a "haunting" in a tavern in the Via Bava in Turin. The proprietor took Lombroso down to the wine cellar, which proved to be covered with broken bottles. And as Lombroso stood there, six bottles floated off the shelf and exploded like bombs on the floor. Even as Lombroso left the cellar, he could hear the sound of breaking glass. In the kitchen, plates flew across the room and shattered, while in the servants' room, a brass meat grinder struck the wall so violently that it was flattened. If it had struck Lombroso, it would have killed him. The odd thing was that, in spite of its violence, the ghost never harmed anyone; heavy vases would miss people's heads by an eighth of an inch, and shatter against the wall.

Lombroso's first theory was that someone in the house was an unconscious "medium" – a person through whom "spirits" can express themselves. He suspected the wife of the proprietor, a skinny, neurotic woman, and suggested that she should go away for a holiday. But the disturbances continued while she was absent. Then Lombroso's suspicions fell on a tall, gangling thirteen-year-old boy, who was suffering from pimples and other physical effects of puberty; he was the only other person who was always present when the disturbances took place. The youth was sent away, and the disturbances instantly ceased.

Now the year 1900 was a time when the theories of Sigmund Freud were becoming known in medical circles. Lombroso reasoned that the turbulent sexual energies of adolescence were somehow responsible for the "poltergeist phenomena", but that the youth himself was totally unaware that he was to blame. In other words, the disturbances were caused by his *unconscious* mind. Of course, this still failed to explain how the unconscious mind can smash plates and bottles; but at least it seemed a step in the right direction. From that time on, most psychical researchers accepted the view that poltergeists are not real "ghosts", but some kind of bizarre effect of the unconscious mind.

Mind Over Matter

But *can* the unconscious mind move material objects? There is strong evidence that it can. In 1934, a professional gambler walked into the office of a psychical researcher named Dr J.B. Rhine and said he believed he could influence the fall of the dice. "Show me," said Rhine. So the two crouched on the floor, and the gambler began to "call his shots" with a remarkable level of success. Soon, dozens of researchers were investigating this strange possibility of mind over matter – it is known as psychokinesis or "PK" – in the laboratory. A Russian housewife named Nina Kulagina discovered she could make matchsticks move around simply by staring at them. And after seeing a film about her, an American researcher named Felicia Parise tried it. She had little success until one day she was told that her grandmother was dying. This gave her a bad shock, and when she reached out for a small plastic bottle, it moved away from her hand. The shock had somehow "shaken up" her unconscious mind, and from then on, she could move small objects simply by staring at them. And this, according to modern psychical research, is a mini-version of the "poltergeist effect", which happens to be far weaker because it is more or less *conscious*. For *really* powerful PK effects, the unconscious needs to operate spontaneously. That, at any rate, is the theory.

Freud's best-known disciple Carl Jung arrived at the same conclusion. He had a female cousin who, at the age of puberty, began to go into trances and speak with strange voices. One day when she was in the house the dining room table split in two with a loud report. There was also an explosion from the sideboard, and when they looked in the drawer, they found that a bread knife had shattered into several pieces. Jung decided that his cousin's unconscious mind was to blame. Jung called these occurrences "exteriorisation phenomena", another name for PK effects.

Years later, he was explaining his idea to the sceptical Freud, and becoming more and more irritated with Freud's stubbornness. Suddenly, said Jung, he experienced a curious burning sensation in his diaphragm, and there was a loud explosion in the bookcase which made Freud jump. "There," said Jung, "*that* is what I meant." "Bosh!" said Freud indignantly. "It is not bosh, and to prove my point, there will be another explosion in a moment." As he spoke, there was another explosion in the bookcase. Jung felt he had proved his point, but Freud always preferred to believe that the case was made of unseasoned wood, and that this was responsible for the cracking noises.

Another eminent Freudian psychiatrist agreed with Jung. He was a Hungarian named Nandor Fodor, and, like Cesare Lombroso, he had encountered poltergeists in the course of his work. He was so fascinated by them that he wrote a history of *The Poltergeist Down the Ages,* noting that the earliest recorded case took place in Bingen, in Germany, in 858 AD, and that the "spirit" showered the farmhouse with stones and shook the walls "as if men were striking them with hammers." It was apparently the farmer himself who was the object of the spirit's "malice", and it followed him around, making his life a misery, and even causing fires. (This is one of the poltergeist's more alarming and dangerous habits.) This poltergeist also developed a voice – which is unusual but not unique – and it denounced the farmer for adultery, and for sleeping with the daughter of his overseer.

And now, suddenly, we can begin to see the familiar pattern emerging. If the girl he seduced was on the verge of puberty, and if she lived in the same house as the farmer – which, in the overcrowded circumstances of the Middle Ages, is quite probable – then it would be understandable that the poltergeist would take out its annoyance on the seducer. Here is a case where Freudian sexual theory and modern psychical research seem to combine to indicate the solution. That, at any rate, was Fodor's view. He even went one further than the usual "unconscious" theory, and suggested something he called "somatic dissociation": "It means that the human body is capable of releasing energy in a manner similar to atomic bombardments. The electron shot out of its orbit . . . is like a bolt of lightning . . . The atom has no power to impart direction to it. A human being has." So, according to Fodor, a disturbed adolescent is like a miniature atomic bomb, with the additional power of *controlling* these strange energies. It is an impressive theory – but does it really cover all the facts?

The Hydesville Haunting

The most famous haunting in the world – and certainly the most influential in terms of its repercussions – took place in the middle of the nineteenth century. The strange case of the Hydesville haunting led to the launching of the movement called Spiritualism, and to the worldwide interest in ghosts and spirits that has persisted down to this day.

In fact, the Hydesville ghost belongs to the poltergeist type.

The Hydesville affair began on 31 March 1848, in a wooden frame house inhabited by a Methodist farmer named James D. Fox, his wife Margaret, and their two daughters, Margaretta, aged fourteen, and Kate, aged twelve. Hydesville is a small township not far from Rochester, New York. James Fox had moved into the house in the previous December. A previous tenant, Michael Weekman, had been disturbed by various loud knocks, for which he could find no cause.

The Fox family was also kept awake by various banging

During his investigation of the powers of Eusapia Paladino, the Italian medium noted for bang-up seances, Professor P. Foa tried to use a photographic plate to register radiations. Eusapia Paladino's spirits apparently resented the interference. As the medium sat in trance outside the curtained cabinet, a hand shot out and tried to snatch the plate. Dr Foa seized the hand as it retreated behind the curtains and felt the fingers, but the hand wriggled loose and hit him squarely.

The spirits then turned their attention to a table, which they sailed over the heads of the company. When one sitter attempted to approach it, the spirits whisked it behind the curtain where it began to break up noisily. Dr Foa saw the table turn over on its side, and one leg snap off. At that point it shot back out of the cabinet and continued to break up noisily under the fascinated gaze of the entire circle. One of the sitters asked for a handshake, and Eusapia Paladino invited him to approach the cabinet. He had hardly reached it when he felt himself attacked by hands and pieces of wood.

The entire circle heard the noises of the blows, and saw the hand moving in the ghostly half-light.

noises in the last days of March 1848; but since it was a windy month, they were not unduly disturbed. On Friday 31 March, the family decided to retire early to make up for lost sleep. Mr Fox went round the house checking the shutters and sashes. The children observed that when he shook the sashes, to see how loose they were, banging noises seemed to reply like an echo.

The whole family slept in two beds in the same room. Just before the parents came to bed, the rapping noises started again. Kate said cheekily, "Mr Splitfoot, do as I do", and began snapping her fingers. To the amazement of the girls, the raps imitated her. Margaret interrupted, "Do as I do", and began to clap. Again, the sounds imitated her. Remembering that the next day would be April the first, the children decided that someone was playing a joke. In her account of what happened, Mrs Fox wrote:

> "I then thought I could put a test that no one in the place could answer. I asked the noise to rap my different children's ages, successively. Instantly, each one of my children's ages was given correctly, pausing between them sufficiently long to individualise them until the seventh [child], at which a longer pause was made, and then three more emphatic little raps were given, corresponding to the age of the little one that died . . ."

Now rather frightened – this was evidently no joke – Mrs Fox asked if it was a human being who was making the raps; there was no reply. "Is it a spirit? If it is, make two raps." Two thunderous bangs followed, so loud that the house shook. She asked if it was an "injured spirit", and again the bangs shook the house. Further questioning revealed that the knocker was a man who died at the age of thirty-one, that he had been murdered in the house, and that he had a wife and five children. Mrs Fox asked if the spirit had any objection to her calling in the neighbours; the raps replied: "No."

The Foxs summoned in about fourteen neighbours. One of these was a man called William Duesler, who assured his own wife that the whole thing was ridiculous and that there could be nothing mysterious about the noises. When he got there, some of the neighbours were too nervous to go into the bedroom, but Duesler was not worried. He went and sat on the bed, and was astonished when Mrs Fox's questions were answered with a rapping noise that made the bed vibrate. (Later writers were to insist that the two children made all the noises by cracking their joints; but it is hard to see how the cracking of joints could make the house shake and cause a bed to vibrate.)

Duesler took up the questioning of the "spirit". By a code of knocks, he established that the entity was a man who had been murdered in the house, a pedlar named Charles B. Rosma, who had been attacked for the $500 he carried. The murder had taken place five years earlier, and had been committed by the man who was then the tenant of the house, a Mr Bell. A maid named Lucretia Pulver later confirmed that a pedlar *had* spent the night in the house, and that she had been sent home; when she returned the next day, the pedlar had gone.

As news of these amazing occurrences spread throughout the community, hundreds of people came to the house. On Sunday 2 April, Duesler learned from the murdered man that his body had been buried in the cellar. This seemed to offer a method of verification, and James Fox and his neighbours took shovels to the cellar – which had an earth floor – and proceeded to dig. At a depth of three feet they encountered water, and abandoned the attempt. But in July, when the water had gone down, they dug again, and at a depth of five feet found a plank; underneath this, in quicklime, there was some human hair and a few bones.

Mr Bell, on being heard that he had been accused of murder by a ghost, indignantly denied it, and produced a testimonial to his good character from his new neighbours in Lyon, New York. The spirit had already prophesied that the murderer would never be brought to justice.

In his account of the case in *Modern Spiritualism*, the sceptical Frank Podmore comments: "No corroborative evidence of the supposed murder, or even of the existence of the man supposed to have been murdered, was ever obtained." This was written in 1902. Two years later, in November 1904, a wall in the cellar of the Fox house collapsed, revealing another wall behind it. Digging between the two walls uncovered a skeleton and a pedlar's tin box. It looked as if someone had dug up the body from its original grave and interred it next to the wall, then built another wall to confuse searchers.

In those days immediately after the first manifestations, a committee was set up to collect the statements of witnesses. Not all the investigators were convinced that the sounds had a supernatural origin; but no one suggested that the Fox family could be responsible. With the family all together in the same room, it was obviously impossible that either the parents or the children could be causing the bangs.

What everyone soon noticed was that nothing happened unless the children were in the house – particularly Kate. A committee of sceptical Rochester citizens came to the house to investigate; they agreed that Margaret was certainly not responsible. A second and third investigation produced the same result. The children were stripped and searched to see if they had some mechanical device for producing the sounds; there was nothing. They were made to stand on pillows with their ankles tied; still the raps occurred.

The children were separated; Kate was sent to stay with her elder sister Leah in Rochester, and Margaretta with her brother

The *Watertown* was a large oil tanker owned by the Cities Service Company. In December 1924 a tragic accident occurred on board the ship. Two seamen, James Courtney and Michael Meehan, were cleaning a cargo tank while the ship was en route to the Panama Canal from the Pacific Coast. Both men were overcome by gas fumes and died. In true maritime tradition they were buried at sea on 4 December 1924.

The next day the phantom faces appeared. The first mate reported to the captain, Keith Tracy, that two faces were following the ship in the water. All the crew, as well as the captain, saw the faces of the two dead men, continually appearing day after day as the ship slowly made its way to the Panama Canal. When the ship docked in New Orleans the captain reported the bizarre events to officials of the Cities Service Company and J.S. Patton, of the company, suggested that the captain try to photograph the faces. The first mate owned a camera and Patton gave a sealed roll of film to the captain, who supervised the loading of the camera, hoping to procure a photograph of the faces.

The captain's hopes were fulfilled. When the *Watertown* set sail for its return voyage the phantoms again appeared. Six photographs were taken of the heads, but the film was not developed until the ship again docked in New Orleans. The film was delivered to J.S. Patton, who sent it to a commercial developer. Five of the photographs showed nothing, but a sixth revealed two heads very distinctly projected on the water dolorously following the ship.

David in Auburn. The "spirits" followed them both. Rapping noises were heard, and people felt themselves touched by invisible hands. In Leah's house, a lodger called Calvin Brown took a mildly satirical attitude towards the spirit, and it began to persecute him, throwing things at him. Mrs Fox's cap was pulled off and the comb pulled out of her hair. When members of the family knelt to pray, pins were jabbed into them. In brother David's boarding house, similar things were happening. It was clear that the murdered pedlar was not responsible for all this – he was back in the Hydesville house, making terrifying gurgling noises and sounds like a body being dragged across the floor. Mrs Fox's hair turned white. One spirit who communicated with Kate claimed to be a dead relative named Jacob Smith. Sister Leah Fish discovered that she could also communicate with the spirits, and began producing messages. One sixteen-year-old girl named Harriet Bebee, who visited the house in Auburn and witnessed the rapping noises, returned to her home miles away and found that the noises had followed her.

The Fox family moved to Rochester, but the manifestations continued. Sometimes the bangs were so loud that they could be heard miles away. Poltergeists had apparently taken over from the original "injured spirit". One day, a visitor named Isaac Post started asking the spirit questions, and was answered by a thunderous barrage of knocks. Then, by means of an alphabetical code, the "spirit" spelled out a message: "Dear friends, you must proclaim this truth to the world. This is the dawning of a new era; you must not try to conceal it any longer. God will protect you and good spirits will watch over you." And now began a series of manifestations that were to become typical of "Spiritualism". Tables moved and rapped with their legs; musical instruments were played by unseen fingers, objects moved round the room. The "spirits" intimated that they would prefer to manifest themselves in the dark – which confirmed the sceptics in their opinion. But other believers decided it was time to put the "spirit's" injunction into operation and "proclaim this truth to the world". On 14 November 1849, the first Spiritualist meeting took place in the Corinthian hall in Rochester.

Many people were convinced that the whole thing was a fraud. Passions rose to a fury, and one occasion, the girls were nearly lynched. But soon the tide began to turn in their favour. They went to New York in 1850 and sat in front of a committee of distinguished American intellectuals and public men for three days, producing rapping noises and messages from the dead, and the committee was convinced. They went on to become the most famous "mediums" in America. In 1861, Kate Fox produced even more remarkable phenomena. Sitting in a locked room, she caused the deceased wife of a banker named Charles Livermore to "materialise" in the room, so the husband could see her clearly, and even exchange a few words with her. While Kate's hands were held, the "spirit" of Estelle Livermore wrote messages on cards, and Livermore acknowledged that this was his dead wife's handwriting. He was so grateful that, as well as paying her generously, he paid for her to take a trip to England, where she became even more famous and successful.

Unfortunately, Margaret and Kate eventually fell on hard times. They quarrelled with their elder sister Leah, (who, unlike her sisters, was still a practising medium) and got together to try and ruin her. Both Margaret and Kate were drinking too much, and Margaret was living in actual poverty. In 1888 they gave interviews in which they claimed that they had made the raps themselves with their big toes, and by cracking their joints. This was obviously absurd, because the loud bangs and crashes in the Fox house could not have been caused by cracking the joints. But it caused a widespread scandal, and opponents of Spiritualism were delighted. But when Margaret was not paid as much money as she expected for these confessions, she withdrew them. Soon after that, both Margaret and Kate died from alcoholic complications. But by that time, Spiritualism had swept across America, and then across the world.

For whatever reason, the Fox sisters began a Spiritualist explosion. People discovered that all they had to do was to sit in a darkened room, preferably with a "medium" present – someone who had already established a communication with the spirits – and the manifestations would usually follow immediately. No apparatus was required, except possibly a few musical instruments. In the Rochester area, more than a hundred "mediums" appeared in the year 1850. In Buffalo, New York, two brothers and a sister named Davenport attended a seance at which the Fox sisters produced their manifestations, and decided to try it themselves – in fact, inexplicable raps and bangs had sounded in their home in the year 1846, two years before the Hydesville manifestations. When Ira, William and Elizabeth Davenport sat in a darkened room, with their hands on a tabletop, the table began to move, raps were heard all over the room, and when Ira picked up a pencil his hand began to write automatically. A few nights later, with witnesses present, all three children were seen to levitate into the air. At their fifth "seance," Ira was instructed – by means of raps – to fire a pistol in the corner of the room. As it exploded, it was taken from his hand, and by the light of the flash, a figure of a man was seen holding it. He vanished a moment later, and the pistol fell to the floor. The man introduced himself – through the code of raps – as John King; he was one of the first examples of a "control" (or master of ceremonies), who acted as intermediary between the medium and the "spirits". "John King" was soon taking over the brothers directly and speaking through their mouths. The Davenport brothers went on to become even more famous than the Fox sisters.

In Dover, Ohio, a well-to-do farmer named Jonathan Koons discovered his own talents as a medium by sitting in a dark room and going into a trance. The "spirits" who spoke through him told him that all his eight children were gifted mediums. They instructed him to build a special house made of logs, sixteen feet by twelve, to be used exclusively for spiritualist activities. There were large numbers of musical instruments – drums, triangles, tambourines, a banjo, an accordion, a harp, a guitar, and so on. The room was dimly lighted by sheets of wet paper smeared with phosphorus. When the mediums – usually Koons and his eighteen-year-old son Nahum – were seated at a small table – with the audience on benches – Koons would play the violin, and the spirits would soon join in, producing the effect of a full orchestra. Witnesses also speak of a heavenly choir joining in. The racket was impressive, and could be heard a mile away. A voice would then deliver a homily, using a speaking trumpet, which floated in the air. A spirit hand floated round the room, touching people and shaking their hands. People came from all over the county to witness these marvels, and the spirits impressed everyone by producing information about strangers that none of the audience could have known.

This was, in fact, one of the most convincing things about the "spirits"; they seemed to have access to all kinds of information. In Boston, the wife of a newspaper editor, Mrs W.R. Hayden, startled the wife of the English mathematician, Augustus de Morgan, by giving her detailed messages from dead friends about whom she could not possibly have known. The result was that Mrs de Morgan invited her to England, where she held seances under "test conditions" in the de Morgans' home. She was loudly ridiculed by the English newspapers, who were convinced that this latest American craze must be based on fraud and deception (which the British were too sensible to swallow), but she convinced most of those who actually saw her. And respectable members of the British middle classes who tried "table-turning" to while away the long evenings were amazed to discover that it actually worked. One journalist wrote a few years later: "In those days you were invited to 'Tea and Table Moving' as a new excitement, and made to revolve with the family like mad round articles of furniture." Even Queen Victoria and Prince Albert tried it at Osborne, and the table moved so convincingly that the Queen had no doubt whatever that no trickery was involved – she decided that the answer must lie in some form of electricity or magnetism.

The initial reaction of scientists to these strange occurrences was incredulity, which slowly turned to fury; they found it incomprehensible that so many people could be "taken in" by this explosion of old-fashioned superstition. It took another twenty years before even the scientists had to recognise that this was more than an outbreak of mass hysteria. Then a group of scientists and intellectuals came together to form the Society for Psychical Research, and it was not long before most of them had to acknowledge that, whatever the explanation, ghosts and poltergeists were undoubtedly more than a figment of the imagination. It was something of an embarrassment to most of them. So when, in 1900, Lombroso propounded his own version of the "unconscious mind" theory, everybody heaved a sigh of relief. It looked as if poltergeists could be explained scientifically after all.

The Dodlestone Poltergeist

But is this true? If poltergeists were really nothing but "spontaneous psychokinesis", you would expect them to appear only where there are emotionally disturbed adolescents in the house, and to be limited to homes where there is a certain amount of misery and tension. In fact, poltergeist disturbances are far more frequent than is generally realised, and occur in all kinds of homes – there is probably one going on within twenty miles of where you are now reading these words; moreover, in many of them, there is not a disturbed adolescent in sight.

In a book called *Vertical Plane*, a teacher named Ken Webster describes how, in 1984, he and his girlfriend Debbie (aged nineteen) moved into a nineteenth century cottage in the village of Dodlestone, near Chester. One morning, as a friend named Nic was helping them paint the kitchen, a set of footprints was seen moving up the wall. A few days later, a stack of cat food tins was found on the kitchen floor. A blast of wind from under the kitchen door – connected to the living room – blew newspapers around like autumn leaves. The poltergeist's favourite activity was stacking things in piles – plates, crockery, cans of food.

Ken Webster had borrowed an old and rather primitive computer at this time, and when he used it in the kitchen, obscure words began to appear on the floppy disk – words he knew he had not typed. When a friend said, "Why not reply?", he at first felt rather silly – but decided it was worth trying. To his astonishment, it worked. The Fox family poltergeist had communicated in a code of raps; this one seemed quite happy to work on the word processor. It identified itself as a man called Thomas Harden, and gave the date as 1546. Oddly enough, he seemed to think that the present date *was* 1546. In fact, it became clear – and we shall find this in case after case – that the ghost *did not know it was "dead"*. One of his first questions was "Why are you breaking into my house?" As absurd as it seems, he seemed to think that Ken Webster was the poltergeist who was haunting *him*.

It all sounded like some kind of a spoof, and at first Ken and Debbie were half-inclined to take this view. What convinced them otherwise was that Thomas Harden used some rather odd words: for example, he said he had been "reethed" at night, and used words like "torablise" and "stincioun". Webster went along to a friend who had studied Middle English at Oxford, and discovered that "reethed" meant "disturbed", "torablise" meant "troubled", and "stincioun" meant "immovable".

The "spirit" showed an unexpected skill with the computer. Unfortunately, when the Society for Psychical Research sent someone to investigate, it became suddenly shy. But one day when the investigators had gone for a walk, and Webster himself was outside, it swiftly typed a message on the disk. The odd thing was that it left it on a part of the disc that took Ken *eight and a half minutes* to access (since this was an ancient model). Yet it did it in less than a minute, an apparent impossibility.

Fortunately, "Thomas Harden" proved to be a fairly good natured soul, telling Ken that he didn't mind him being in his house. He continued to make his presence felt, throwing bits of metal pipe around when Ken and Debbie had visitors – they were warm when picked up – and making the upper floor of the house shake as if in an earthquake. He also bent the handle of a copper pan at right angles, then straightened it a day or so later. Oddly enough, although the handle was rusted, and might be expected to show signs of having been bent, it looks totally undamaged, as if Harden had some Uri Geller-like power over metals.

Finally, as if becoming bored with the whole thing, Thomas Harden went away. Or perhaps he got someone to come and exorcise his house and get rid of his strange twentieth-century intruders. At all events, Ken and Debbie still live in the cottage, and now all is peaceful.

We can see that the Dodlestone case seems to contradict the "disturbed adolescent" theory. Ken was twenty-nine, and although Debbie was only nineteen, she was certainly not "disturbed". But both Ken and Debbie felt oddly depleted and lethargic during Thomas Harden's tenancy, as if he was using their energy to manifest himself.

Harry Price, one of the most famous of pre-war investigators, disagreed with the "spontaneous PK" theory; he stated his conviction that poltergeists are genuine spirits or ghosts, who need to use the energy of human beings to manifest themselves. His view is now highly unfashionable. But cases like Douglass Deen, the Turin poltergeist and the Dodlestone manifestations seem to suggest that he could have been right after all.

The Bell Witch

In general, the poltergeist is harmless. Some heavy object big enough to kill a human being may fly within an inch of someone's head – yet it always misses. There have, however, been a few rare cases in which someone has been seriously hurt, or even killed. The best known of these is known as the Bell Witch.

It began in 1817, in the farm in Tennessee where John Bell lived with his wife and nine children; one of these was a twelve year old girl, Betsy, and it gradually became clear that she was the "focus" of the disturbances. These began in the usual way, with scratching noises and knockings (poltergeist effects always work their way up from small effects to large ones). There were sounds like rats in the walls and an invisible dog clawing at the floor. Then stones began to be thrown, and the bedclothes were whipped off beds; if the children tried to hold them on, they were slapped by an invisible hand. Strange whistling sounds gradually developed into a poltergeist voice which sounded not unlike a parrot with asthma. Whenever the disturbances were at their height, Betsy became pale, and often fainted (or went into a trance).

Now the "voice" – or rather, voices – developed, some of them quoting extracts from sermons, others using foul language. The major entity identified itself as a witch called Old Kate Batts. She declared that she was a tormented spirit who would make John Bell suffer and kill him in the end. And this is precisely what the poltergeist proceeded to do. It made his tongue swell until it filled his mouth; it struck him violently in the face; it sent him into convulsions. During all this time the "witch" shrieked with demonic laughter. On 19 December 1820, the long-suffering man was found unconscious in his bed. The "witch" declared that she had poisoned him, and in the medicine cabinet they found a bottle of a dark-coloured liquid which, when tried on the cat, killed it instantly. Bell died the next day.

In the following year, there was a loud explosion in the kitchen chimney, and the witch's voice shrieked: "I am going and will be gone for seven years." And so she was. Seven years later, the scratching noises started again; but this time they soon stopped, and the "Bell witch" was gone forever.

Nandor Fodor, the Hungarian psychologist who believed that poltergeists are explosions of "Freudian" energy, is convinced that John Bell had made an incestuous attack on Betsy, and that this was the cause of all the trouble; Betsy's repressed hatred finally exploded into attacks of "recurrent spontaneous psychokinesis". Yet there is one obvious objection to this theory. "Talking poltergeists" take considerable pleasure in embarrassing their victims, especially in public. If John Bell *had* committed incest – or even tried to – with Betsy, it seems unlikely that Old Kate Batts would not have said so in the most specific and crude language.

On the whole, the notion that poltergeists are spirits who do not know they are dead (psychical investigators call them "earthbound spirits") seems to fit the facts as well as any.

• chapter two •

ANCIENT GHOSTS

Every country in the ancient world believed in ghosts: Babylon, Egypt, Israel, Greece, Rome, China, Japan. The trouble with the ghost stories that survive is that they are so fantastic and absurd that no sensible person can take them seriously. The Babylonians believed in a female ghost called Lamashtu, who snatched babies from their mothers' breasts, Namtaru, a plague demon who ruled the underworld, and "Rabisu the Croucher", who lurked in dark corners and leapt out to terrify unwary passers-by. It does not take much common sense to see that these were the inventions of ignorant and superstitious people who were afraid of the dark and had only the crudest ideas about medicine. The ancient Greeks believed in a kind of vampire-cannibal called the lamia, a beautiful girl who would lure men with her physical charms, then eat them. The ancient Chinese believed in vampires with red eyes, razor sharp claws, and green hair, who enjoyed eating dead bodies, and could re-create a body from a skull or a few bones. The Japanese were firmly convinced – and to some extent still are – of the existence of "were-foxes", beautiful female spirits who transform themselves into foxes.

Any modern investigator would dismiss these stories as pure superstition – possibly based on some grain of truth that has been so embroidered and distorted that it is now impossible to guess what it was. On the other hand, there are some ghost stories dating from ancient times that sound perfectly plausible – exactly like hundreds of other similar stories collected by the Society for Psychical Research.

The Unhappy Ghost of Pausanias

The Spartan general Pausanias took part in the great war between the Greeks and the Persians, which took place in the fifth century BC, and defeated the Persians in the great naval battle of Plataea in 479. That made him famous, and he went on to other successes. But according to the historian Thucydides, success made him conceited and arrogant, and after capturing Byzantium, he behaved so tyrannically that the Spartans asked him to come home and explain himself. This made Pausanias so furious that he approached the Persian king Xerxes and offered to betray his own people. Eventually, proof of his treachery came from a messenger who had kept a letter to a Persian go-between. (The letter had a PS: "Kill the messenger so he can't talk", and the messenger, wondering why previous messengers had failed to return, opened it up.) Pausanias fled to the temple of Athena, and took shelter in a small building next door. His pursuers walled him in, and allowed him to starve to death.

The result of this, according to an ancient chronicle, was that the ghost of Pausanias began to haunt the temple, and made such terrifying noises that the priestess was forced to send for a magician, who finally persuaded the ghost to go away.

And why is this story any more believable than stories about Greek vampires who eat men alive, and Japanese ladies who turn themselves into foxes? Because it sounds as if the ghost of Pausanias behaved exactly like a poltergeist. There are many stories of men and women who died under tragic circumstances, and who are not aware that they are dead – these are known as "earthbound spirits". There are also many examples of such spirits being persuaded to go away by a medium – we shall later discuss the case of the Enfield haunting of 1977 in which this happened. So there is nothing at all improbable about the story of the ghost of Pausanias.

The Chain-rattling Ghost of Athens

At which point, let us look at what is probably the very first story about a haunted house. It is told in a letter by the Roman author Pliny the Younger (61–114 AD).

According to Pliny, a certain large house in Athens remained permanently untenanted because it was haunted by the ghost of a filthy old man who rattled chains and made moaning noises. A few sceptics who spent the night in the haunted house were terrified out of their wits. Finally, the place began to turn into a crumbling ruin.

At this point, the stoic philosopher Athenodorus came on a visit to Athens and saw the house, and decided that it looked an ideal place for solitary study. On discovering that the rent was absurdly low, he decided to move in at once. The owners of the house told him frankly why it had remained untenanted, but Athenodorus said he was not afraid of ghosts. All he needed from them, he said, was a table and a few chairs, a bed and a lamp.

That same day he moved in. But out of curiosity – and possibly a little nervousness – he decided to spend the first night awake.

For several hours, all was quiet, and Athenodorus became absorbed in his writing. Then he heard the sound of rattling chains, which approached closer and closer. When he looked up, he saw the apparition of a filthy old man, who was beckoniong to him with his finger. Athenodorus waved his hand dismissively and went back to his writing. The ghost began to moan and rattle his chains. Finally, Athenodurus gave in – it was impossible to concentrate – and followed the old man down the dusty corridor and out into the garden. There the ghost walked as far as a dense clump of shrubs and vanished.

Athenodrus made a pile of stones to mark the spot, and went back to his room, where he slept peacefully for the rest of the night.

The next day he told the Athenian authorities what he had seen. Magistrates returned with him to the spot in the garden, and workmen began to dig. Several feet down they struck something hard. Cautiously clearing away the earth, they found a skeleton wearing rusty chains and shackles. These were so ancient that they fell off when the skeleton was moved.

The bones were buried in a proper grave with appropriate ceremonies, and the haunting ceased forthwith.

True or false? Most readers will unhesitatingly say: false. Why? Because there are so many improbabilities – to begin with, a ghost that moans and rattles chains, and a philosopher who is so cool that he ignores the ghost and goes on writing.

But now look at the story more closely. The philosopher Athenodorus died in the year 7 AD, about half a century before the birth of Pliny the Younger, and only sixteen years before the birth of Pliny the Elder, the latter's uncle and guardian. And since first-century Rome was full of Greeks, and every educated Roman regarded Athens as a spiritual home, the story was almost certainly passed on to Pliny by someone who was alive at the time it happened. In other words, it was not ancient history, but a fairly recent happening.

Second, some ghosts *do* make noises, as we have seen in the case of the Hydesville poltergeist, which declared it was a pedlar who had been murdered by the previous tenant. Whether the noise made by the ghost of the old man was really a rattling of chains or the usual banging and crashing of the poltergeist is another matter. What we *can* see is that if the ghost of the old man behaved like the Hydesville poltergeist, somebody would very quickly embroider the story to add rattling chains.

As to the main absurdity in the story – the coolness of the philosopher – it is easy to see that this would also be added soon after the event, probably the very next day. Perhaps Athenodorus added it – or at least, told the magistrates that he had kept his head and refused to panic. And, men being what they are, this would soon be converted into the story of the philosopher coolly waving the ghost away. In fact, no one would do such a thing, least of all a philosopher.

So altogether, we can see that the story of the haunted house of Athens is perfectly credible, and almost certainly happened. One more detail adds to its credibility. If it had been invented, its author would almost certainly have invented a reason for the old man being chained and shackled – he had been kept prisoner in the house by a wicked relative who had claimed his fortune, and who had told everyone that the old man had gone on a business trip and failed to return. But there is no such embroidery; the story is left unfinished because, in fact, no one could recall anything about the old man . . .

• chapter three •

GHOSTS OR TAPE RECORDINGS?

The Cotgrave Colliery Ghost

In the autumn of 1989, a nineteen-year-old miner, Gary Pine, was working alone in a remote part of Cotgrave Colliery in Nottinghamshire when the moving conveyor belt began to make odd groaning noises. Gary assumed that something had got stuck in the roller and went to look; as he did so, he saw a man standing a few yards away, dressed in a black helmet and dark overalls, and realised with a shock that *he* was groaning. Gary's natural assumption was that somebody was playing a joke and trying to scare him; then, as he watched, the man walked through a pile of sacks and disappeared down a dead end. At that point, Gary realised he had seen a ghost – the shock was so severe that he had to take time off from work to recover. For weeks after the sighting, miners would only go into the "haunted" area in pairs.

Their attitude is understandable but – in the view of students of psychical research – quite unnecessary. No ghost in all the recorded history of sightings has ever been known to harm anyone (as distinguished from poltergeists – who, as we have seen, can *very* occasionally be harmful). In fact, according to the most widely held theory, they would be incapable of harming anyone because they are no more "real" than old films.

The Hampton Court Ghost

Consider, for example, the case of the haunted Long Gallery at Hampton Court, where the ghost of a woman with long flowing hair is reported. It is identified as Lady Catherine Howard, the wife of Henry the Eighth. This is what Peter Underwood, president of the Ghost Club, has to say about her in his *Gazeteer of British Ghosts.*

> Perhaps the most famous ghost at Hampton Court is that of Lady Catherine Howard who came here in 1540, a lovely girl of eighteen, as bride of the fat, lame and ageing monarch. After little more than a year ugly rumours began to circulate and it was said that she behaved little better than a common harlot, both before and after her marriage. The night before she was arrested, her first step to the block, she broke free from her captors and sped along the gallery in a vain effort to plead for her life with her husband. But Henry, piously hearing vespers in the chapel, ignored her entreaties and she was dragged away, still shrieking and sobbing for mercy. As you go down the Queen's Great Staircase you can see on the right-hand side the low-roofed and mysterious corridor containing the room from which Queen Catherine escaped and to which she was dragged back, her screams mingling weirdly with the singing in the chapel. Her ghost re-enacts the grisly event on the night of the anniversary, running shrieking through what has come to be known as the "Haunted Gallery". Those who have heard and seen her ghost include Mrs Cavendish Boyle and Lady Eastlake, together with many servants at the palace. All the witnesses say the figure has long, flowing hair but it usually disappears so quickly that no one has time to observe it closely.
>
> A hundred years ago the "Haunted Gallery" was locked and used as a storage room for pictures but adjoining chambers were occupied as a grace and favour apartment by a titled lady who has recorded that once, in the dead of night, she was awakened by

> an appalling and ear-piercing shriek which died away into a pulsating silence. Not long afterwards she had a friend staying with her who was awakened by a similar dreadful cry which seemed to come from the "Haunted Gallery". After the Gallery was opened to the public an artist sketching some tapestry was startled to see a ringed hand repeatedly appear in front of it but he hurriedly sketched the hand and ring. The jewel was later identified as one known to have been worn by Catherine Howard.

All this sounds like a typical piece of absurd "spooky" gossip. But the psychical investigator Joan Forman had a personal experience of the manifestation. She had walked down the Long Gallery and stood by the chapel door when she experienced a sensation "of utter misery and extreme physical coldness". And when she received a letter from Mrs F. Kerridge of Towcester, she was fascinated to learn that Mrs Kerridge had experienced it even more strongly. Mrs Kerridge described how, as she reached the door of the royal pew, she encountered "such an agony of distress" that she stepped backwards. She tried to walk through the door three or four times, and each time had the same experience. "One went through a cloud – invisible but tangible to one's senses. Two clouds really: one agony was at the door of the antechamber, one in the Pew itself – with nothing between." What she was "picking up", Mrs Kerridge believed, was the misery of Catherine Howard as she battered at the door, and the misery of the King who was seated inside, tormented by guilt and his still-powerful attachment to her.

That sounds plausible – Catherine *was* beheaded the following year, and it seems a reasonable assumption that her spirit might relive the traumatic experience. But Henry himself lived on for another six years. Why should his spirit haunt the spot? The answer, Joan Forman reasoned, is that it wasn't Henry's ghost that Mrs Kerridge felt in the royal pew; it was a kind of *recording* of his misery, just as the sense of agony at the door of the pew was a recording of Catherine's agony.

In fact, the "tape recording" theory of ghosts was first put forward around 1900 by the eminent scientist Sir Oliver Lodge. He noticed the interesting fact that many people do *not* see ghosts that are perfectly visible to other people – in some cases, two people can be in the same room, and only one of them sees the ghost. Why should that be? Perhaps, thought Lodge, for the same reason that some people can dowse for underground water with a hazel twig while others are completely insensitive to water. In other words, one of them is picking up "vibrations" like a radio set and the other is insensitive to them. Which in turn suggests that a ghost is some kind of "broadcast" or recording, not a real spirit. Lodge theorised that powerful tragic emotions, like those associated with murder or suicide, may be absorbed by the walls of houses in which such events have occurred, and sensitive people can "pick them up", just as bloodhounds can scent things that no human being would notice.

The Ghost in Hunting Kit

The same theory occurred to a retired Cambridge don, T.C. Lethbridge, more than fifty years later. When Lethbridge was a student at Cambridge, he was certain he had seen a ghost in the rooms of a friend. He had been about to leave, late at night, when a man wearing a top hat stepped into the room. Assuming he was a college porter with a message, Lethbridge said goodnight; the man did not reply. The next day Lethbridge asked his friend what the porter had wanted. His friend looked at him in amazement, and insisted that no one had entered the room. It was only then that Lethbridge recalled that the "porter" had been dressed in a kind of hunting kit – except it was not red, but grey. He concluded that he had seen the ghost of some previous occupant of the rooms.

Half a century later, Tom Lethbridge was sitting on a Devon hillside, looking down on the garden of his next-door neighbour, an old lady who claimed to be a witch. In the garden he could see the "witch", and a few feet away, a tall old lady dressed in grey, old fashioned clothes. He was so curious about her that he later asked his neighbour about her visitor. The old lady looked puzzled; and replied that she had been alone at the time. Then, as Lethbridge described the woman, she said: "Ah, you've seen my ghost."

Lethbridge's first idea was that the tall woman had been

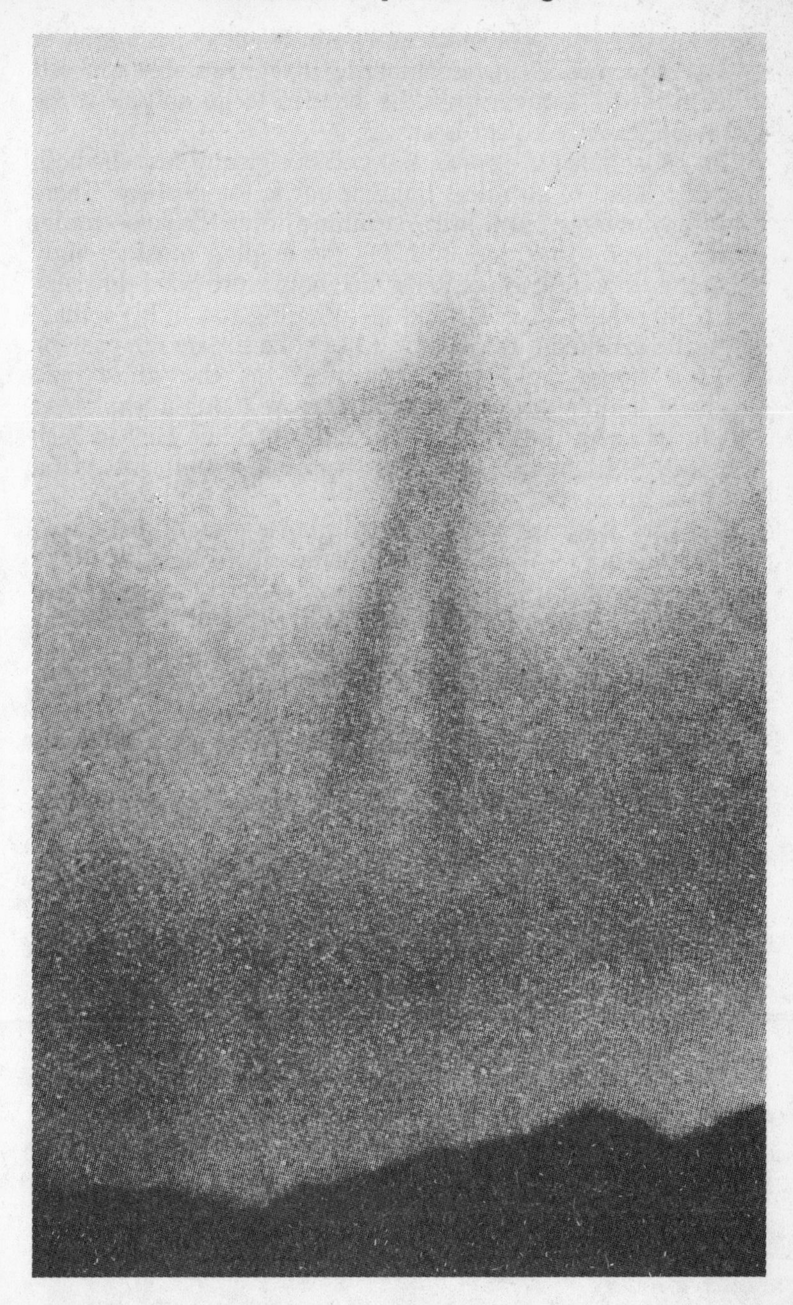

Harz Mountains, Germany – The Spectre of Brocken

some kind of "thought projection" – in other words a kind of television picture. Then, remembering that ghosts are supposed to reappear on anniversaries, he decided to go and sit at the same spot exactly a year later.

The ghost failed to appear. But Lethbridge and his wife both noticed a kind of electrical tingling in the atmosphere. There was a tiny underground stream running down the lane – under a drain cover – and they both felt the tingling most strongly when they stood on top of it. (In fact, both were good dowsers, and Lethbridge had even used his dowsing rod in his archaeological work, to locate volcanic dikes.) The stream ran past the "witch's" house, and Lethbridge realised that the "ghost" had also been standing directly over it. This, he thought, explained why he had seen the ghost and the witch had not. He had been "connected" to the spot by the underground stream, just as if it had been an electric wire.

And now it struck him that both ghosts – the "huntsman" and the tall lady – were probably "tape recordings" and that, for some reason, the picture had "recorded" in black and white instead of in colour, which is why both wore grey.

But what were they recorded *on*? Lethbridge concluded: the electrical field of water. His Cambridge friend's rooms had looked out on the river and were damp. Lethbridge came to believe that all "tape recorded" ghosts are seen in damp places.

At first the theory may sound far-fetched. But then, if you had told a contemporary of Shakespeare that one day sounds would be captured on tape, or on the wax bumps on a record, he would have thought you were insane. If we can accept the notion of sound (and video pictures) being captured on iron oxide tape, is it so unlikely that strong emotions could be captured on an electrical field of water?

So according to Lethbridge, the ghost of the coal miner at Cotgrave Colliery, and the spectre of Catherine Howard in the Long Gallery at Hampton Court (also close to a river) were "tape recordings". There can be no doubt that this theory fits many famous hauntings. Ghosts are often in "black and white", and they fade like a television being switched off.

The RAF Ghost

Yet it must be admitted that there are a few hauntings that are more difficult to explain. One of them was still going on in 1990 at RAF Linton-on-Ouse, Yorkshire, the main training school for jet pilots. The "spirit" – of an officer in flying kit – has been seen by many people in the control tower. Flight Lieutenant Mark Byrne was in there with twenty-one-year-old Brenda Jenkinson one night when both saw the figure – a man about six feet tall – walking across the room towards the approach room. It looked grey and shadowy, and vanished suddenly into thin air. The phantom has been seen by several other members of staff. But the RAF – which gave a press conference to talk about the ghost – believes it knows its identity. In 1959, Warrant Officer Walter Hodgson, from Hull, died at the age of thirty-eight, and his family got permission to put up a plaque in his memory outside the control tower. A few years ago, the plaque was moved inside. From then on, the "ghost" began appearing in the tower.

At the press conference, Squadron Leader Mike Brooks explained his own belief that the "spirit" of Walter Hodgson was upset about the removal of his plaque. But if he is right, then the ghost cannot be a "tape recording", which obviously couldn't care less whether a plaque were inside or out. Does this mean that Lethbridge was wrong about "tape recordings"? Not necessarily. Everyone who has studied hauntings knows that there seem to be be two types of ghost. One behaves like a tape recording or a television picture, fading away after a few moments; the other seems to respond to the presence of other people in the room, and often looks perfectly normal and solid, like a real person. Most of this latter type behave like people who do not know they are dead.

The Ghost in the Changing Room

The novelist Wilbur Wright had an experience with this kind of ghost. In 1941, when he was in the RAF at Hemswell, he returned from leave late one night and walked into a hangar to get some cigarettes from his locker. It was in darkness, and when he switched on the light, he saw a Leading Aircraftman named Stoker groping around in his locker. When Wright asked what he was doing, Stoker replied: "I can't find my bloody gloves." Wright located his cigarettes and thought no more of it.

The next morning at breakfast he asked if anything had happened in his absence, and was told that the bomber in which Stoker was a gunner had been shot down over Dortmund. "Stoker had a lucky escape then?" "Oh no – he went down with the rest. There was trouble before he took off – he couldn't find his flying gloves and kept moaning about it . . ."

Wright was so shocked that he reported sick and was unable to sleep for nights. It was only later that it struck him that the hangar had been in total darkness before he switched on the light and that he should have realised then that there was something odd about a man looking for his gloves in the dark.

It is, of course, possible that Stoker was a "tape recording". But Wilbur Wright's account makes it sound as if, like Warrant Officer Hodgson, Stoker was a real "spirit". In fact, cases of this sort – people who are "seen" by relatives or friends soon after death – make up the great majority of reported sightings of ghosts.

There are hundreds of similar recorded cases in the archives of the Society for Psychical Research. What follows is a small but typical selection.

Some Typical Cases

On 21 October 1893, Prince Victor Duleep Singh, a son of a maharajah, went to bed in a Berlin hotel, where he was staying together with Lord Carnarvon. Before switching off the light, he looked across the room at a framed picture that hung on the opposite wall. To his surprise, he saw the face of his father, looking at him with an intent expression. Thinking that the picture might resemble his father, he got out of bed to see; in fact, it showed a girl holding a rose and leaning on a balcony.

Prince Victor described the experience to Lord Carnarvon the next morning. Later the same day, he received a telegram announcing that his father had died of a stroke the previous day. The prince had seen his father's face at the time when the maharajah was lying unconscious after the stroke, a few hours before he died.

On the night of 16 October 1902, the wife of a railway guard woke up about 3 am for a drink of water. She was alone in bed, because her husband was on night duty, and the room was dimly lighted by a gas mantle. As she looked into the water, she saw a clear image of goods wagons smashing into one another, and observed which of them was most damaged. She was worried about her husband, in case he had had an accident. At nine the next morning he returned home, and she told him what she had seen. He told her that there *had* been an accident on the line that night, and it had happened just as she had seen.

The odd point about this case is that her husband had passed the scene of the accident twice: once at the time his wife had seen her "vision" in the glass of water, and again four hours later, when his train was on its way back. But when he passed it for the first time, it was dark and he could not see what was happening. At 7 am it was light, and he had then been able to see the scene clearly – as his wife had seen it in the water. Of course, her husband may have seen far more subconsciously than he was aware of seeing. But if this was telepathy, then he had managed to convey to his wife far more than he was aware of seeing.

The next case is perhaps one of the most famous ever recorded by the SPR. On 9 July 1904, the novelist Rider Haggard suffered such a bad nightmare that his wife shook him awake. In his dream, he had seen his daughter's black retriever dog, Bob, lying on its side among the undergrowth beside some water. Its head was at an unnatural angle, and it seemed to be trying to tell him that it was dying.

The next morning at breakfast Haggard told his daughter Angela about his dream. She was quite unworried because she had seen Bob the previous evening and he was safe and well. It was only later in the day that they learned that Bob was missing. Four days later, the dog's body was found floating in the nearby river. It had been struck by a train on the night Haggard had dreamed about it. He was able to work out the precise time the accident had taken place – a few hours before he had awakened from his nightmare.

On 19 March 1917, Mrs Dorothy Spearman was in her room in a hotel in Calcutta, feeding her baby son. Her little daughter was also in the room. She felt there was someone behind her, and looked round to see her half-brother, Eldred Bowyer-Bower, standing there; he was an officer in the Royal Flying Corps. He looked perfectly normal, and Mrs Spearman assumed he had been posted to India and come to see her. She told him that she would put the baby down, and then they could have a long talk. But when she had finished tucking in the baby, her half-brother had vanished. Her daughter did not appear to have seen anyone. She learned later that her half-brother had been shot down over the German lines at about the time she had seen him.

On 7 December 1918, Lieutenant J.J. Larkin, an RAF officer, was writing letters in the billet when he heard someone walking up the passage outside. Then the door opened, and his friend Lieutenant David McConnel shouted: "Hello boy!" Larkin turned and saw McConnel standing there, holding the doorknob in his hand. He said: "Hello, back already?" and McConnel replied "Yes, had a good trip". He had been ferrying a plane to a nearby aerodrome. Then McConnel closed the door with a bang and clattered off.

When Larkin learned several hours later that McConnel had crashed that afternoon, he assumed that it must have been after he had seen him. In fact, McConnel had been killed at roughly the same time that Larkin saw him at the door.

The next case has also become famous, and is regarded as one of the strongest pieces of evidence for survival after death. In June 1925, James Chaffin of Davie County, North Carolina, dreamed that his father stood by his bedside, wearing an old black overcoat, and told him: "You will find the will in my overcoat pocket." The father, James L. Chaffin, had died four years earlier, leaving his farm to his third son Marshall, and nothing to his wife or other three sons. The will had not been contested, since there seemed no reason to do so.

The next morning, James Chaffin hurried to his mother and asked about his father's old black overcoat; she told him it had been given to his brother John. He found the coat at John's house and examined it carefully. Sewn into the lining of the inside pocket – which his father had indicated in the dream – he found a roll of paper stating: "Read the 27th chapter of Genesis in my daddy's old Bible."

Taking a neighbour as witness, James Chaffin went back to

his mother's house, and unearthed the old Bible. In the 27th chapter of Genesis there was another will – made later than the one that left everything to Marshall – dividing the property between the wife and four sons. The first reaction of Marshall Chaffin was to contest the will, assuming it to be a forgery. But once he examined it, he had to admit that it was obviously genuine. Ten witnesses testified that it was in old Chaffin's handwriting. So the property was divided according to the wishes of the second will.

Like Marshall Chaffin's, the reader's first reaction is to suspect skulduggery. But the Canadian member of the SPR who heard of the case hired a lawyer to investigate it, and the genuineness of the will was established beyond all doubt. The significance of the 27th chapter of Genesis is that it contains the story of how Jacob deceived his blind father Isaac into granting him the inheritance of his brother Esau. This thought had apparently come to old Chaffin not long before his death, and he made the new will. But instead of having it properly witnessed, he inserted it in the Bible, no doubt expecting it to be found after his death – together with its implied criticism of his son Marshall. Unfortunately, the Bible was decrepit, and it may have been that the Chaffin family was simply not religiously inclined; so after four years, it seems the old farmer had to draw attention to his change of heart . . .

Mrs Crowe's *Night Side of Nature* has a whole chapter devoted to similar cases, in which important messages are delivered by dreams or apparitions. She tells, for example, of a butcher who dreamed that he was going to be attacked and murdered on his way to market by two men dressed in blue. He decided to go to market with a neighbour, and when he came to the place where the attack had taken place in his dream, saw the two men in blue waiting there . . . But all she tells us by way of detail is that the butcher's name was Bone and that he lived in Holytown. This can hardly be regarded as "confirmatory detail". The records of the SPR contain many equally melodramatic cases. But they took the trouble to get signed statements from all concerned, and the result is far more convincing. In a typical case of 1869, a couple, identified as "Mr and Mrs P", were lying in bed in a dimly lighted room when "Mrs P" saw a man dressed as a naval officer standing at the foot of the bed. Her husband was dozing, and she touched his shoulder and said: "Willie, who is this?" Her husband roared indignantly: "What on earth are you doing here, sir?" The naval officer said reproachfully, "Willie!", and, as

"Mr P" leapt out of bed, walked across the room, and disappeared into the wall. "Mrs P" said he looked like a solid human being, and that as he passed a lamp on his way across the room, he threw a shadow.

Realising that they had seen a "ghost", "Mrs P" began to wonder if it foreboded some disaster to her brother, who was in the navy. When she mentioned this to her husband, he said: "No, it was my father." "P"'s father had been dead for some years.

After this visitation, "Mr P" became seriously ill for several weeks. When he recovered, he told his wife that he had been in financial trouble for some time, and before seeing the apparition, he had decided to take the advice of a certain individual which, he now realised, would have ruined him and probably landed him in jail. He was convinced that the "ghost" had come to warn him not to do it.

Intrinsically, this case is no more convincing than that of Mr Bone of Holytown. But the SPR obtained signed depositions from "Mr and Mrs P", and from two friends to whom "Mrs P" had told the story immediately after it had happened. It is still possible to dismiss it as a dream or a "collective hallucination", or simply as a downright lie. But the signed statements make this seem at least unlikely.

An interesting point about the experience is "Mrs P"'s comment that the figure looked quite solid and normal – most "ghosts" do – and that it cast a shadow. This obviously suggests that it was made of some kind of solid substance, like the "materialisations" that appeared in the seance room.

A "warning" of a different kind seems to have been involved in a case that came to be known as the "red scratch" case. It involved a commercial traveller (identified as "FG") who was in his hotel room in St Joseph, Missouri, in 1876, when he became aware of someone sitting at the table. It was his sister Annie, who had died of cholera nine years earlier. She looked exactly as she had when alive, except that she had a bright red scratch on her right cheek. As "FG" sprang to his feet, his sister vanished.

He was so shaken that he took a train straight back to his parents' home in St Louis. When he told them about the scratch, his mother fainted. When she recovered, she told them that she had accidentally made the scratch on the face of the corpse. She had covered it up with powder, and never mentioned it to anyone.

A few weeks later, the mother died, "happy in the belief that she would rejoin her favourite daughter". Her son obviously took the view that the purpose of the apparition was to prepare her mother for her own death. This is another theme that runs fairly constantly through reports of apparitions and "death-bed visions" collected by the SPR. Sir William Barrett was later to devote a book to them, and its opening case is typical of the kind of thoroughness the SPR brought to its investigations.

Barrett's wife was an obstetric surgeon in the Maternity Hospital at Clapton in North London. A woman she calls "Mrs B" was in labour and suffering from heart failure. As Lady Barrett was holding her hands, she said: "It's getting dark." Her mother and husband were sent for. Then "Mrs B" looked at another part of the room and said: "Oh, lovely." "What is lovely?" "Lovely brightness – wonderful things." Then she exclaimed: "Why, it's father!" Her baby was brought in for her to see, and she asked: "Do you think I ought to stay for baby's sake?" She looked towards her "father", and said: "I can't stay." When her husband had arrived, she looked across the room and said: "Why, there's Vida!" Vida was her younger sister, who had died two weeks earlier. But the death had been kept from "Mrs B", so as not to upset her. She died soon after. Lady Barrett, the matron and the husband and mother all vouched that she seemed to remain conscious of the dead relatives up to the time of her death. With his usual thoroughness, Barrett obtained a letter verifying all this from the mother. It is the first of a number of cases cited by Barrett in which people on the point of death have "seen" relatives whom they did not know to be dead. Barrett points out that there is no known case of a dying person "seeing" someone who is still alive.

Sir Oliver Lodge, who was twice president of the SPR, was himself to supply one of the most convincing cases of "communication with the dead"; it is recorded in his book *Raymond*.

On 8 August 1915, Sir Oliver Lodge received a message from a Boston medium, Leonore Piper, containing an obscure reference to a poem by the Roman poet Horace, about a tree being struck by lightning. Lodge interpreted this as a warning of some disaster. The message purported to come from Frederick Myers, who had been dead for fourteen years. A week later, Lodge heard that his youngest son Raymond had been killed in the Ypres campaign.

After this, a number of mediums relayed messages that

purported to come from Raymond, but Lodge remained unconvinced – most of them were of the "Having a lovely time" variety. But in the following month, Lodge's wife was taken by a friend to a seance by a remarkable medium, Mrs Osborne Leonard. Neither the medium nor Lady Lodge knew one another by sight, and they were not introduced. Nevertheless, Mrs Leonard announced that she had a message from "Raymond", who stated that he had met many of his father's friends since death; asked to name one of them, Raymond replied "Myers".

Another "message" from Raymond was relayed to Lady Lodge via a male medium called Vout Peters; in it, "Raymond" spoke about a photograph showing himself in a group of people, and referred to a walking stick. The Lodges knew nothing about such a photograph. Two months later, the mother of one of Raymond's fellow officers wrote to say that she had a group photograph including Raymond, and offered to send a copy. Before this arrived, Lodge himself visited Mrs Leonard, and when her "control" "Feda" announced Raymond's presence, he took the opportunity to ask about the photograph. Raymond explained that it had been taken outdoors, and mentioned that someone had wanted to lean on him. When the photograph arrived a few days later, it showed a group of officers outside a billet. Raymond, sitting in the front row, has a cane resting on his leg, and the officer sitting behind him is using Raymond's shoulder as an arm rest.

Lodge's book gives many more examples of evidence of Raymond's "survival"; but, as he points out, this one is particularly convincing because it involves two mediums, both of whom spoke of the photograph before Lodge knew of its existence – thus ruling out any possibility of telepathy.

To conclude this chapter, here is a final example of a type of phenomenon so beloved by Mrs Crowe and other early writers on the "supernatural": the full-scale haunting.

In February 1932, the grandchildren of a chimney-sweep named Samuel Bull refused to go to sleep, insisting that there was someone outside the door of the cottage. (They were sleeping in a downstairs room, recovering from influenza.) Their mother, Mary Edwards, looked outside the door, but there was no one there. Soon afterwards, she and the children saw the figure of Samuel Bull – who had been dead since the previous June – walk across the room, up the stairs, and through the door of the room in which he had died. (This was closed.) They all screamed. This was the first of many appearances of the dead man at his cottage in Oxford Street, Ramsbury, Wiltshire.

The "ghost" was apparently aware of the presence of his family, for he twice placed his hand on the brow of his invalid wife Jane, and once spoke her name. Samuel Bull – who had died of cancer – looked quite solid, and could be seen so clearly that the children noticed the whiteness of his knuckles, which seemed to be protruding through the skin. They also noticed that the expression on his face was sad. After the first appearance, the family no longer felt alarmed – the children seemed "awed" rather than frightened. They assumed that the ghost was looking sad because of the miserable conditions they were living in – the cottage was damp and some rooms were unfit for habitation. On the last two occasions on which he appeared, Samuel Bull no longer looked sad, and Mrs Edwards assumed that this was because the family was to be re-housed in a council house.

The family was already on the move when the two investigators from the SPR arrived, but the local vicar had already interviewed the family and recorded their accounts of what took place. The investigators were understandably upset that they had not been told about the case earlier, but their conversations with witnesses, and the evidence of the vicar, left them in no doubt that the haunting was genuine.

On the whole, then, the evidence seems to suggest that while *some* ghosts are "tape recordings", others behave exactly like real people who do not realise they are dead.

• chapter four •

THE GHOSTLY "DOUBLE"

Soon after the Society for Psychical Research was formed in 1882, a three man team set about collecting accounts of what they called "phantasms of the living" – that is, people who are seen miles away from the place where they actually are at the time. Phantasms of the Living *is a huge book – more than two thousand pages – and it contains hundred of accounts of strange sightings. Many of these do not involve the dead. For example, a Mrs Sarah Hall was sitting at her dinner table with her husband and another couple when all of them saw another Sarah Hall standing by the sideboard. Mr Hall said with astonishment: "Why, it's Sarah!" – at which the "phantom" Mrs Hall vanished. As far as is known, she never reappeared, and the story has no sequel. The phantom was of the type that psychical researchers call "doppelgangers" or doubles, and they seem to be – as Lethbridge suggested – some kind of "mental projection" or television picture.*

The Doppelganger of a Girl in a Hurry

Doppelgangers are surprisingly common: in fact, I can personally vouch for a recent case.

During the time of the Napoleonic Wars, a German named Wesermann had been trying experimentally to send his apparition to various people. One night he decided to try instead to transmit the image of someone else. A lady who had died five years before was to appear to a Lieutenant N. in a dream at about 10:30 pm.

As it happened, Lieutenant N. had not yet gone to bed but was visiting a friend, Lieutenant S.. The two were chatting, and N. was just about to go to his room when the kitchen door opened and, in the words of S., "a lady entered, very pale . . . about five feet four inches in height, strong and broad in figure, dressed in white, but with a large black kerchief which reached to below the waist. She . . . greeted me with the hand three times in complimentary fashion, turned round to the left toward Herr N., and waved her hand to him three times; after which the figure quietly, and again without any creaking of the door, went out."

The case is interesting because the behaviour of the apparition was suited to the circumstances, which were not foreseen by the agent. He had expected N. to be asleep. The apparition behaved like a real person in greeting both men.

A few days ago, my part-time secretary, Pam, had a strange experience. Something had gone wrong with her car, making her late for her job at the local training college. When she finally arrived, a colleague asked her casually why she had gone away again. Puzzled, she asked him what he meant. "Well, you arrived half an hour ago, and now you're coming back again . . ." When she assured him that she had only just arrived, he looked at her as if she was joking.

Three more colleagues had also seen her, and assured her that she *had* arrived earlier, looking pale and distracted, and carrying the same folder that she always carried. One of them had spoken to her, but she had hurried past without answering.

Oddly enough, they had all seen her wearing her usual black coat. But on that day she was, in fact, wearing another coat for the first time.

Pam admitted that, as she was anxiously trying to start her car, she was thinking about the office. In some strange way, her anxiety had projected an image of herself which was seen by three colleagues at work. It was the Germans who gave such "projections" the name "doppelgangers" or "doubles", and

At the age of twenty-two the German poet Johann Wolfgang von Goethe had completed his studies in Strasbourg and was about to return home. While in Strasbourg he had fallen in love with the daughter of a pastor in a nearby village. He loved her but didn't want to be tied.

He paid one last visit to his Fredericka before leaving the town. "When I reached her my hand from my horse, the tears stood in her eyes and I felt sad at heart," he wrote in his autobiography. Then, as he rode away, he had a strange vision. "I saw, not with the eyes of the body, but with those of the mind, my own figure coming toward me on horseback, and on the same road, attired in a suit which I had never worn – pike gray with gold lace. As soon as I shook myself out of this dream the figure had entirely disappeared . . . eight years afterward, I found myself on the very road, to pay one more visit to Fredericka, in the suit of which I had dreamed."

Although the phenomenon of seeing one's doppelganger is traditionally regarded as a death omen, Goethe did not interpret his experience in that way. "However it may be with matters of this kind generally, this strange illusion in some measure calmed me at the moment of parting."

there are hundreds of well-authenticated examples in the literature of psychical research.

The Doppelganger of John Cowper Powys

One of the most impressive concerns two novelists: John Cowper Powys and the American Theodore Dreiser.

One day in 1929, Powys had spent the early evening with Dreiser in his New York apartment. As he left he remarked: "You'll be seeing me later this evening." Dreiser thought he was joking, for Powys lived fifty miles away. But a few hours later, Dreiser looked across the room, and saw Powys standing inside the door. He jumped to his feet saying: "John! Come on in and tell me how you did it." But as Dreiser advanced towards him, Powys vanished.

Dreiser rushed to the telephone and rang Powys's number in upper New York State. Powys answered. And when Dreiser told him that he had just appeared in the room, Powys merely said: "I told you I'd see you later." Next time Dreiser saw him, he firmly refused to discuss the incident.

It is highly probable that the reason he refused to discuss it is that he had no idea how he did it. When he left Dreiser, he probably felt in a certain "mood", and was sure that he could do it. But he couldn't explain exactly how.

The Beard Case

One of the most famous incidents of "projection" occurred in the 1890s, and was studied by the Society for Psychical Research in London. A student named Beard was engaged to a girl called Miss Verity. One night, after reading a book on the unknown powers of the mind, Beard decided that he would

Harry Price, Psychic Researcher

try to "appear" to his fiancée. He sat in his armchair and tried to "will" himself to appear in her room. Suddenly, he felt as though he could not move his limbs. He "woke up" some time later sitting in the armchair. The next day, Miss Verity told him that she had seen him the previous evening in her bedroom. In fact, her younger sister had also awakened and seen him. A moment later, Beard had vanished.

Beard repeated this strange performance on a second occasion, when he not only "appeared" to Miss Verity's elder sister (who was staying in the house), but even touched her hair and took hold of her hand – apparently his own hand felt quite solid.

Beard made the interesting comment that he made a peculiar mental effort "which I cannot find words to describe . . . but which I can now at times set in motion at will." Obviously, Powys had also learned to make this mental effort. And my secretary somehow did it accidentally because she was worried about being late for work.

Perhaps one of the most interesting comments made by Beard is that when he was suddenly unable to move his body, he thought that this was because he had fallen into a "hypnotic trance".

Hypnosis seems to be able to release powers of which we are normally unaware. One student of the mystery said that it is as if we possess *two selves*, one of them the "normal everyday self", and the other a *deeper* self of which we are unaware – like the part of the iceberg below water. When a person is hypnotised, the "everyday self" goes to sleep, but the deeper self remains awake, and can do the most remarkable things. So it is quite possible that the "peculiar effort" made by Beard may have been a kind of self-hypnosis, and that he was then able to appear to his fiancée.

The Case of Emilie Sagée

In one famous case of a "doppelganger", a French schoolteacher named Emilie Sagée kept losing her job because her "double" would appear and frighten the pupils. One day, when Emilie was in the school garden, she looked through a window and noticed that the schoolmistress had left the class for a moment, and that the girls were being noisy. Suddenly, the girls were amazed to see Emilie sitting in the schoolteacher's chair – while they could see the real Emilie standing out in the garden. One girl was brave enough to approach the "double" and touch her; she said that Emilie's flesh felt like muslin.

Poor Emilie was obviously incapable of controlling these "projections", and after losing job after job, she finally committed suicide.

One obvious explanation of the mystery is that it is some kind of telepathy. Most of us have had the experience of knowing what someone else is thinking, or conveying out thoughts to others. Perhaps we also have some mysterious power of conveying our *images* to others, like a television picture. Yet this seems to be contradicted by the fact that Beard was able to touch the hair of Miss Verity's sister, and hold her hand. Does the "telepathy" include an illusion of touch? Or is it possible that our "strange unknown powers" include the power to send our solid bodies elsewhere in the world?

Phantom Hitchhikers

In the 1970s, stories about phantom hitchhikers began to appear in newspapers all over the world. The story told by motorcycle policeman Mahmood Ali of Peshawar, India, is typical. He gave a lift to a pretty girl dressed in white. Before they reached the place to which she had asked to be taken, she had vanished from the back of his motorbike. Investigation revealed that the girl had been involved in a fatal accident at the spot where he had picked her up; he identified the photograph of the victim as that of his hitchhiker, "eyelash for eyelash".

Michael Goss is a respected psychical researcher who, in the early 1980s, was asked to look into the evidence for such cases, and his book *The Evidence for Phantom Hitch-Hikers* has a deeply sceptical tone; he points out the basic similarities in many of the stories, and argues that this is a typical example of the modern "folk legend". Yet he is forced to admit that a number of cases cannot be dismissed in this way. One concerns a twenty-six-year-old carpet-fitter named Roy Fulton, whom Goss himself interviewed on tape. On a Friday night in 1979, after playing in a darts match at Leighton Buzzard, Fulton drove back towards Dunstable through Stanbridge. In a dark lane he saw a man thumbing a lift, and pulled up; the man opened the door and got in. When Fulton asked where he was going, the man merely pointed ahead. Five minutes later, Fulton started to offer the man a cigarette, and found that he had vanished. He braked hard and looked in the back – there was no one there. So he drove fast to a pub in Dunstable, had a large scotch, then reported the incident to local Police Inspector Rowland.

Goss originally suspected that Fulton may have invented the story for the sake of notoriety, but a check with the local police, and with the publican who had served the badly shaken man the whisky, convinced him that it was genuine.

Are phantom hitchhikers ghosts, or simply doppelgangers projecting their "images" to another place? The obvious objection to this theory is that you would not expect a doppelganger – which seems to be some kind of mental image – to open a door. But then, when drivers offer a lift, *they themselves* usually lean over and open the door, often in order to ask the hitchhiker where he wants to go to. So where phantom hitchhikers are concerned, it is worth keeping an open mind.

• chapter five •

VAMPIRES

Do vampires exist? The question sounds absurd – surely no sane person could take the idea seriously?

But then, the study of psychical research makes it clear that there are more things in heaven and earth than the average sceptic would be willing to grant. In the opening chapter of this book we considered the case of the "haunted boy of Washington", which seems to show fairly conclusively that some kind of "possession" can happen. We have also seen that the "Exorcist" case started with poltergeist effects, which seems to suggest that the "spirit" that claimed to be a demon was just an ordinary poltergeist telling lies. Poltergeists are like juvenile delinquents; they *love* causing trouble and confusion. And, as we shall see in this chapter, some stories about "vampires" make them sound very much like poltergeists operating according to slightly different rules.

It should be explained that the common idea of vampires, derived from films with Bela Lugosi and Christopher Lee, is almost completely mythical. *That* all started as recently as 1816, when Lord Byron was driven out of England by outraged public opinion, and began a lifetime of exile on the continent. He took with him his personal physician, a rather self-assertive young man named John Polidori. Most people have now heard the famous story of how Byron and Polidori, together with the poet Shelley and Shelley's wife Mary, stayed together in a villa overlooking Lake Geneva, and began talking about ghost stories. The result was that Mary Shelley wrote *Frankenstein*, and Byron began a tale called "The Vampyre". He wrote only a few pages, then gave up. But the competitive Polidori pushed on to complete his own tale "The Vampyre". This was about a sinister nobleman named Lord Ruthven (pronounced "Rivven") who charms his way into the affections of young ladies, only to leave their bodies drained of blood. It appeared in 1819 and caused a sensation – dozens of imitations immediately appeared, and it was turned into a popular opera by Marschner. Polidori's subsequent career was not a success, and he committed suicide two years later, at the age of twenty-five.

In 1849, a hack writer named James Rymer produced a vast serial novel called *Varney the Vampire*, which went on to become a bestseller. This improved on Polidori's formula, with its tall, cadaverous figure with eyes like "polished tin" and hideous fangs. This in turn was improved on by Bram Stoker in his masterpiece *Dracula* (1897) which has become the source of all modern stories about vampires. His Count Dracula was based on a real historical character, a king of Wallachia called Vlad the Impaler – the name derives from his unpleasant habit of impaling people on pointed stakes. Vlad was a sadist, and his death in battle in 1477 caused widespread relief.

But how did the legend of the blood-drinking vampire begin? The story first reached Europe soon after 1718, when Charles VI, Emperor of Austria, drove the Turks out of Eastern Europe, which they had dominated for the past four centuries, marching in and out of Transylvania, Wallachia and Hungary and even conquering Constantinople (1453). Don John of Austria defeated them at the great sea battle of Lepanto (1571), but it was their failure to capture Vienna after a siege in 1683 that caused the break-up of the Ottoman empire. During the earlier stages of this war between Europe and Turkey, Vlad the Impaler struck blow after blow against the Turks, until they killed and beheaded him in 1477. When the Turks were finally defeated, two hundred and forty-one years later, their conquerors were intrigued to hear strange stories about dead people who could cause death to the living. Such stories had been known to travellers in Greece down the centuries. There the vampire was known as the *vrykolakas*, and on 1 January 1701, a French botanist named Pitton de Tornefort had visited the island of Mykonos and been present at a gruesome scene of dissection. An unnamed peasant, of sullen and quarrelsome disposition, was murdered in the fields by persons unknown. Two days after burial, his ghost was reported to be wandering around at night, overturning furniture and "playing a thousand roguish tricks". Ten days after his burial, a mass was said to "drive out the demon" that was believed to be in the corpse, after which the body was disinterred, and the local butcher given the task of tearing out the heart. His kncwledge of anatomy seemed to be defective, and he tore open the stomach and rummaged around in the intestines, causing such a vile stench that incense had to be burned. In the smoke-filled church, people began shouting "Vrykolakas" and alleging that some of the smoke poured out of the corpse itself.

Even after the heart had been burned on the seashore, the ghost continued to cause havoc, until the villagers finally burnt the corpse on a pyre.

De Tornefort takes a highly superior attitude about all this, convinced that it is simply mass hysteria. "I have never viewed anything so pitiable as the state of this island. Everyone's head was turned; the wisest people were stricken like the others." Although the year is only 1701, de Tornefort's attitude is that of a typical French rationalist of the eighteenth century.

Attitudes began to change after 1718, as the highly circumstantial accounts of vampires began to reach Western Europe – just how precise and circumstantial is illustrated by a report, known as *Visum et Repertum* (Seen and Discovered), which dates from 1732, and was witnessed by no less than five Austrian officers.

The vampire epidemic of 1730–35 seems to have started at the village of Meduegna, near Belgrade, through a young soldier named Arnold Paole, who returned from active service in Greece in 1727. He told the girl to whom he was betrothed that he had been attacked at night by a vampire in Greece, but had located its grave and destroyed it – which should have removed the curse. However, he died, and then was seen around the village after dark. Ten weeks later, after several people claimed to have seen him, or dreamed about him and felt strangely weak the morning after, his body was disinterred by two army surgeons and the sexton and his assistants. The body still had blood on its mouth. It was covered with garlic, which is supposed to be a protection against vampires, and a stake had been driven through the heart.

Six years later, there was an epidemic of vampirism at

Meduegna, and this time several distinguished doctors investigated; the medical report was signed on 7 January 1732, by Johannes Flickinger, Isaac Seidel, Johann Baumgartner and the lieutenant colonel and sub-lieutenant from Belgrade. They testified to examining fourteen corpses, all listed and described, including a girl of ten. Only two of the fourteen – mother and baby – were found in a normal state of decomposition, all the others being "unmistakably in the vampire condition". It is not recorded what was done, but presumably the corpses were burned or impaled.

There are even earlier accounts of the walking dead. The French expert on vampires, Jean Marigny, remarks:

"Well before the eighteenth century, the epoch when the word 'vampire' first appeared, people believed in Europe that the dead were able to rise from their graves to suck the blood of the living. The oldest chronicles in Latin mention manifestations of this type, and their authors, instead of employing the word 'vampire' (which did not yet exist) utilised a term just as explicit, the word 'sanguisugae' (Latin for leech, bloodsucker). The oldest of these chronicles date from the twelfth and thirteenth centuries, and, contrary to what one might expect, are not set in remote parts of Europe, but in England and Scotland."

He goes on to cite four cases described by the twelfth century chronicler William of Newburgh, author of *Historia Rerum Anglicarum*. These are too long to cite here (although they can be found in full in Montague Summers' *The Vampire in Europe*). The first, "Of the extraordinary happening when a dead man wandered abroad out of his grave", describes a case in Buckinghamshire, recounted to the chronicler by the local archdeacon. It describes how a man returned from the grave the night after his burial, and attacked his wife. When this happened again the following night, the wife asked various neighbours to spend the night with her, and their shouts drove the ghost away. Then the ghost began to create a general disturbance in the town, attacking animals and alarming people. That he *was* a ghost, and not a physical body, is proved by the comment that some people could see him while others could not (although they "perceptibly felt his horrible presence"). The archdeacon consulted the bishop, Hugh of Lincoln, who – on the advice of various learned men – suggested that the body should be dug up and burnt to ashes. Then he decided this would be "undesirable", and instead wrote out a

Devotees place flowers and a cross on the tomb of Sarah Ellen Roberts, the legendary 'vampire woman' of Blackburn, Northern England, she was buried in Peru in 1949 when her husband was unable to do so in England.

charter of absolution. When the tomb was opened, the body proved to be "uncorrupt", just as on the day it was buried. The absolution was placed on his chest and the grave closed again; after that, the ghost ceased to wander abroad.

One of William of Newburgh's other accounts sounds slightly more like the traditional vampire in that the ghost – of a wealthy man who had died at Berwick on Tweed – had an odour of decomposition which affected the air and caused plague. The body was exhumed (it is not recorded whether it was undecayed) and burned.

Stories like these have the touches of absurdity that might be expected from an ecclesiastical chronicler of that period; yet their similarity to the other chronicles cited suggests that they have some common basis. The same applies to another work, *De Nugis Curialium* by Walter Map (1193), also cited at length by Summers.

All these cases took place long before Western Europe heard tales of vampires from former Turkish dominions, and in only one of them is there is any suggestion of blood-drinking. But in most ways, the revenants behave very much like Peter Plogojowitz and the vampires of Medvegia. They haunt the living, climb into bed with people when they are asleep, and then throttle them, leaving them drained of energy. And when the bodies are disinterred, they are found to be undecayed. It seems very clear that there is no basic difference between the vampires of 1732 and the revenants of the twelfth century. And when we look more closely into the accounts of the vampires, we discover that they are energy-suckers rather than blood suckers. Peter Plogojowitz has fresh blood on his mouth, but it is merely a matter of hearsay that he sucked the blood of his victims – the account mentions only throttling. Otherwise, these earlier revenants behave very much like the paranormal phenomenon known as the poltergeist.

Two sixteenth century cases also bear a close resemblance to the later vampire legends. One is known as known as the Shoemaker of Breslau, and is to be found in Henry More's *Antidote Against Atheism* of 1653. This describes how, on 21 September 1591, a well-to-do shoemaker of Breslau, in Silesia – one account gives his name as Weinrichius – cut his throat with a knife, and soon after died from the wound. Since suicide was regarded as a mortal sin, his wife tried to conceal it, and announced that her husband had died of a stroke. An old woman was taken into the secret, and she washed the body and bound up the throat so skilfully that the wound was invisible. A priest who came to comfort the widow was taken to view the corpse, and noticed nothing suspicious. The shoemaker was buried on the following day, 22 September 1591.

Perhaps because of this unseemly haste, and the refusal of the wife to allow neighbours to view the body, a rumour sprang up that the shoemaker had committed suicide. After this, his ghost began to be seen in the town. Soon it was climbing into bed with people and squeezing them so hard that it left the marks of its fingers on their flesh. This finally became such a nuisance that in the year following the burial, on 18 April 1592, the council ordered the grave to be opened. The body was complete and undamaged by decay, but "blown up like a drum". On his feet the skin had peeled away, and another had grown, "much purer and stronger than the first". He had a "mole like a rose" on his big toe – which was interpreted as a witch's mark – and there was no smell of decay, except in the shroud itself. Even the wound in the throat was undecayed. The corpse was laid under a gallows, but the ghost continued to appear. By 7 May, it had grown "much fuller of flesh". Finally, the council ordered that the corpse should be beheaded and dismembered. When the body was opened up, the heart was found to be "as good as that of a freshly slaughtered calf". Finally, the body was burnt on a huge bonfire of wood and pitch, and the ashes thrown into the river. After this, the ghost ceased to appear.

Paul Barber, citing the case in *Vampires, Burial and Death*, agrees that "much in this story is implausible", but points out that so many details – notably the description of the body – are so precise as to leave no doubt "that we are dealing with real events".

But what are these "real events"? Before we comment further, let us consider another well known case from the same year, 1592 (which is, of course, more than a century earlier than the famous vampire outbreak in eastern Europe). This is also to be found in More, and concerns an alderman of Pentsch (or Pentach) in Silesia named Johannes Cuntze (whose name More latinises to Cuntius). On his way to dinner with the mayor, Cuntze tried to examine a loose shoe of a mettlesome horse, and received a kick, presumably on the head. The blow seems to have unsettled his reason; he complained that he was a great sinner, and that his body was burning. He also refused to see a priest. This gave rise to all kinds of rumours about him, including that he had made a pact with the devil.

As Cuntze was dying, with his son beside the bed, the casement opened and a black cat jumped into the room and leapt on to Cuntze's face, scratching him badly; he died soon after. At his funeral on 8 February 1592, "a great tempest arose", which continued to rage as he was buried beside the altar of the local church.

Before he was buried, there were stories that his ghost had appeared and attempted to rape a woman. After the burial, the ghost began to behave like a mischievous hobgoblin, throwing things about, opening doors, and causing banging noises so that "the whole house shaked again" – on the morning after these events, animal footprints or hoofmarks were found outside in the snow. His widow had the maid sleeping in her bed; the ghost of Cuntze appeared and demanded to be allowed to take his proper place beside his wife. And the parson of the parish (who is mentioned as the chronicler of these events) dreamed that Cuntze was "squeezing" him, and woke up feeling utterly exhausted. The spirit was also able to cause a nauseating stench to fill the room.

The conclusion is much as in the story of the shoemaker of Breslau. Cuntze was finally disinterred on 20 July, five months after his burial, and was found to be undecayed, and when a vein in the leg was opened, the blood that ran out was "as fresh as the living". After having been transported to the bonfire with some difficulty – his body had apparently become as heavy as a stone – he was dismembered (the blood was found to be quite fresh) and burnt to ashes.

So the earlier vampire stories are very clearly about poltergeists, not blood-drinkers. And the Greek and Eastern European cases bear a strong resemblance to stories of "demonic possession".

If we can once concede the possibility of "psychic invasion", as well as the possibility of "spirits", then the notion of vampires suddenly seems less absurd. In *The Magus of Strovolos,* an American academic, Kyriacos C. Markides, has described his friendship with a modern Cypriot mystic and "magus", Spyros Sathi, known as Daskalos, who lives in Nicosia. Daskalos takes the actual reality of spirits for granted. It also becomes clear that Daskalos takes "possession" for granted, and Markides tells a number of stories, in some of which he was personally involved.

There are, Daskalos claims, three kinds of possession: by ill-disposed human spirits, by demonic entities, and by elementals (the latter being human thoughts and desires which have taken on a life of their own). And he goes on to describe a case of spirit possession of the first type. Daskalos was approached by the parents of a girl who claimed that she was being haunted by the spirit of her dead fiancé. Although they had lived together, she had refused to allow him to possess her until they were married. He died of tuberculosis, haunted by unfulfilled cravings. "Each night before she would go to bed he would semi-hypnotise her and induce her to keep the window of her room open. He would then enter inside a bat and would come to her. The bat would wedge itself on her neck and draw blood and etheric (energy)." The local priest told Daskalos how to deal with it. He must wait in the next room, and when he heard the bat entering, should go in and quickly shut the window; then, since the bat would attack him, he must stun it with a broom. Then he must wrap the bat in a towel and burn it in a brazier (stove). Daskalos did this, and as the bat burned, the girl screamed and groaned. Then she calmed down and asked: "Why were you trying to burn me?" The "haunting" ceased thereafter.

Daskalos told another story that has elements of vampirism. On a journey in southern Greece he had encountered another girl who was being haunted by a former lover. A shepherd who had been in love with her had died in a motor accident. Five years later, when looking for some goats, the girl saw the shepherd – whose name was Loizo – and he followed her, finally making her feel very sleepy so she felt obliged to sit down. He then "hypnotised" her, and caused her to experience intense sexual pleasure. When she reported the incident, she was medically examined and found to be a virgin. But three days later the shepherd came to her bed and made love to her. Medical examination revealed she was no longer a virgin. Daskalos noticed two reddish spots on her neck. "He kisses me there, but his kisses are strange. They are like sucking, and I like them."

Daskalos claimed that, two days later, he saw the shepherd coming into the house and greeted him. Loizo explained that he had wanted the girl for many years, and had never had sexual relations with a woman – only with animals like donkeys and goats. Now he was possessing her, he had no intention of letting her go. He refused to believe it when Daskalos told him he was dead. Daskalos warned him that if he persisted in possessing the girl, he would remain "in a narcotized state like a vampire". His arguments finally convinced the shepherd, who agreed to go away.

The doctor who examined the girl believed that she had torn the hymen with her own fingers; Daskalos seems to accept this, but believes that Loizo made her do this.

These two cases, taken in conjunction with the others we have considered, offer some interesting clues about the nature of the vampire. According to Daskalos, the "earthbound spirit" of the dead fiancé was able to enter an ordinary bat and then to suck her blood. This was an expression of his sexual desire, his desire to possess her. There had been many cases in the history of sex crime of so-called "vampirism". In the early 1870s, an Italian youth named Vincent Verzeni murdered three women and attempted to strangle several more. Verzeni was possessed by a powerful desire to throttle women (and even birds and animals). After throttling a fourteen-year-old girl named Johanna Motta, he disembowelled her and drank her blood. Verzeni admitted that it gave him keen pleasure to sniff women's clothing, and "it satisfied me to seize women by the neck and suck their blood". So it is easy to imagine that the earth-bound fiancé mentioned by Daskalos should enjoy drinking the girl's blood. But we can also see that his desire to "possess" her was also satisfied in another way – by somehow controlling her imagination. As the bat was burning, the girl cried out, "Why are you trying to burn me?"

Again, in the case of Loizo, we can see that the shepherd had entered the girl's body and taken possession of her imagination, enough to cause her to tear her own hymen with her fingers. This implies – as we would expect – that the lovemaking was not on the physical level, since Loizo possessed no body.

All this has an interesting implication. The act of lovemaking seems to involve a paradox, since it is an attempt at interpenetration by two bodies, an attempt which is doomed to failure by their separateness. Plato expresses the paradox in an amusing myth. Human beings were originally spherical beings who possessed the characteristics of both sexes. Because their sheer vitality made them a challenge to the gods, Zeus decided that they had to be enfeebled. So he sliced them all down the centre, "as you and I might slice an apple", and turned their faces back to front. And now the separated parts spent their lives in a desperate search for their other half, and they ceased to constitute a challenge to the gods.

It is also clear that, in its crudest form, the male sexual urge is basically a desire for "possession", and that the act of physical penetration is an act of aggression. (Most writers on *Dracula* have noted that it is basically a rape fantasy.) As a man holds a woman in his arms, he experiences a desire to absorb her, to blend with her, and the actual penetration is only a token union. So we might say that a "vampire" like Loizo is able to achieve what every lover dreams about: a possession that involves total interpenetration.

The notion of vampirism that begins to emerge from all this is simple and (provided one can accept the notion of "earthbound spirits") plausible. Daskalos told Markides that those who commit suicide may become trapped in the "etheric of the gross material world", unable to move to the higher psychic planes. A suicide dies in "a state of despair and confusion", and "may vibrate too close to the material world, which will not allow him to find rest". He becomes a "hungry ghost", wandering in and out of the minds of human beings like a man wandering through a deserted city. Yet he is incapable of influencing his involuntary host, or of making his presence felt, unless the host also happens to be on the same "wavelength" and to share the same desires.

Vampirism, then, involves the notion that "earthbound spirits" are attracted by the vitality of the human aura, and may do their best to share it. A book called *Hungry Ghosts*, by the journalist Joe Fisher, makes this point with great force. Fisher had written a book about reincarnation, in the course of which he had become convinced of its reality. One day, after being interviewed on radio in Toronto (where he lives), he received a phone call from a woman who explained that she had accidentally become a mouthpiece of "discarnate entities". She was being hypnotised in an attempt to cure her of leukaemia, and various "spirit guides" had begun speaking through her mouth. (Myers points out that a "spirit" can only enter a body when the usual "tenant" is absent, a point to note when considering that early accounts of vampires involve attack *during sleep*.)

The first time Fisher went to her house, a "spirit" named Russell spoke through her mouth with a reassuring Yorkshire accent, and told him that he had a female "guide", a Greek girl named Filipa, who had been his mistress in a previous existence three centuries earlier. This struck Fisher as plausible, since he had always felt some affinity with Greece. He began attending the seances regularly, and devoting some time every morning to relaxing and trying to contact Filipa. Eventually he succeeded; buzzing noises in his ears would be followed by a feeling of bliss and communication. Filipa was a sensual little creature who liked to be hugged, and Fisher implies that, in some sense, they became lovers. It broke up his current love affair; his live-in girlfriend felt she was no match for a ghost.

Other people at the seances were told about their "guides" or guardian angels. One guide was an ex-RAF pilot named Ernest Scott, another an amusing cockney named Harry Maddox. Fisher's disillusionment began when, on a trip back to England, he decided to try and verify Ernest Scott's war stories – with no doubt whatever that they would prove genuine. The airfield was certainly genuine; so was the squadron Ernest claimed to have belonged to; the descriptions of wartime raids were accurate; so were the descriptions of the squadron's moves from airfield to airfield. But there had been no Ernest Scott in the squadron, and a long search in the Public Record Office failed to throw up his name. Fisher went back to Canada in a bitter mood and accused Ernest of lying. Ernest strenuously denied it. Anyway, he said, he was due to reincarnate in another body, so had to leave . . . The "guide" Russell later told Fisher that Ernest had been reborn in England, and gave the name of the parents and date of birth. Oddly enough, when Fisher checked on this it proved to be accurate. He even contacted the parents, who were intrigued, but decided they had no wish to get more deeply involved.

With Russell's approval, Fisher tried to track down the farm in Yorkshire where Russell claimed he had lived in the nineteenth century. Here again, many of the facts Russell had given about the Harrogate area proved to be accurate; but again, the crucial facts were simply wrong. It seemed that Russell was also a liar. And so, upon investigation, was the lovable World War One veteran Harry Maddox. His accounts of World War One battles were accurate; but Harry did not exist.

Finally, Fisher took his search to Greece. In spite of his disillusion with the other guides, he had no doubt whatever that Filipa was genuine. She possessed, he states early in the book, "more love, compassion and perspicacity than I had ever known". The problem was that all his attempts to locate Theros – a village near the Turkish border – in atlases or gazetteers had failed. Yet that could be because it had been destroyed by the Turks in the past three centuries. But a town called Alexandroupoli, which Filipa had mentioned, still existed. After a long and frustrating search for the remains of Theros, Fisher went to Alexandroupoli, a city that he assumed had been founded by Alexander the Great. But a brochure there disillusioned him. Alexandroupoli was a mere two centuries old; it had not even existed at the time when he and Filipa were supposed to have been lovers . . . Like the others, Filipa was a liar and a deceiver.

In a chapter called "Siren Call of the Hungry Ghosts", Fisher tries to analyse what has happened to him. And the answer seems simple. He had been involved with what Kardec called "earthbound spirits", spirits who either do not realise they are dead, or have such a craving to remain on earth that they remain attached to it. These earthbound spirits or, in Tibetan Buddhist phraseology, *pretas* or "hungry ghosts", are individuals whose minds, at the point of physical death, have been incapable of disentangling from desire. Thus enslaved, the personality becomes trapped on the lower planes even as it retains, for a while, its memory and individuality. Hence the term "lost soul", a residual entity that is no more than an astral corpse-in-waiting. It has condemned itself to perish; it has chosen a "second death". He quotes Lt-Col. Arthur E. Powell, in a book called *The Astral Body*: "Such spooks are conscienceless, devoid of good impulses, tending towards disintegration, and consequently can work for evil only, whether we regard them as prolonging their vitality by vampirising at seances, or polluting the medium and sitters with astral connections of an altogether undesirable kind."

He also cites the modern American expert on "out of the body" journeys, Robert Monroe: "Monroe tells of encountering a zone next to the Earth plane populated by the 'dead' who couldn't or wouldn't realise they were no longer physical beings . . . The beings he perceived kept trying to be physical, to do and be what they had been, to continue physical one way or another. Bewildered, some spent all of their activity in attempting to communicate with friends and loved ones still in bodies or with anyone else who might come along."

The conclusion would seem to be that the vampire cannot be dismissed as a myth. But the reality of vampirism has very little in common with the Dracula legend. There is no fundamental difference between vampires and poltergeists – except that, fortunately, vampire phenomena seem to be far more infrequent.

• chapter six •

PHANTOMS

The Phantom Drummer of Tedworth

The amazing story of the Phantom Drummer has become the most famous of British hauntings. It was recorded by an Oxford clergyman named Joseph Glanvil, who was so intrigued by the case that he went to investigate it personally.

The story begins in a day in mid-March 1661, when a magistrate named John Mompesson was visiting the small town of Ludgershall in East Wiltshire. While he was talking to the town bailiff, he heard in the street outside the noisy racket of a drum that almost drowned their conversation. When he asked what it was, the bailiff explained that it was an idle beggar who claimed he had a pass, signed by two eminent magistrates, giving him permission to attract attention to himself with his drum. He had also tried to use his pass to claim public assistance. The bailiff added that he thought the pass was a forgery, but had no proof. Since Mompesson knew most of his fellow magistrates, he sent the constable to bring the drummer to explain himself.

The beggar, a middle-aged man named William Drury, seemed perfectly confident of himself – in fact, rather arrogant. When Mompesson asked him by whose authority he plied his trade in Wiltshire, the man answered that he had good authority, and produced a pass signed by Sir William Cawly and Colonel Ayliff. A single glance told Mompesson that it was a clumsy forgery – he happened to know the handwriting of both men – and he ordered the beggar to hand over his drum. Then he told the constable to take him off to jail and bring him before the next sitting of the local bench.

Drury quickly lost his arrogance, and admitted that the pass was a forgery. And as the constable started to lead him away, he begged for the return of his drum. But Mompesson, who seems to have been an officious sort of man who enjoyed using his authority, told him that he could have the drum back if the local magistrate discharged him. And despite Drury's pleas, he refused to let him have the drum.

In fact, the local constable seems to have allowed Drury to escape. But the drum stayed behind.

A few weeks later, the bailiff of Ludgershall sent the drum to Mompesson's house in Tedworth. Mompesson was just on his way to London. When he came back he found the house in uproar. For three nights, there had been violent knockings and raps all over the house – both inside and out. That night, when the banging started, Mompesson leapt out of bed with a pistol and rushed to the room from which the sound was coming. It moved to another room. He tried to locate it, but it now seemed to be coming from outside. When he got back into bed, he was able to distinguish drumbeats among the rapping noises.

For the next two months, it was impossible to get to sleep until the middle of the night; the racket went on for at least two hours every night. It stopped briefly when Mrs Mompesson was in labour, and was silent for three weeks – an indication that the spirit was mischievous rather than malicious. Then the disturbances started up again, this time centring around Mompesson's children. The drumbeats would sound from around their beds, and the beds were often lifted up into the air. When the children were moved up into a loft, the drummer followed them. The servants even began to get used to it: one manservant saw a board move, and asked it to hand it to him; the board floated up to his hand, and a joking tug of war ensued for twenty minutes or so, until the master ordered them to stop. When the minister came to pray by the children, the spirit showed its disrespect by being noisier than usual, and leaving behind a disgusting sulphurous smell – presumably to imply it came from Hell. Scratching noises sounded like huge rats.

Things got worse. During the next two years lights were seen, doors slammed, unseen skirts rustled, and a Bible was burnt. The creature purred like a cat, panted like a dog, and made the coins in a man's pocket turn black. One day, Mompesson went into the stable and found his horse lying on its back with its hind hoof jammed into its mouth; it had to be pried out with a lever. The "spirit" attacked the local blacksmith with a pair of pincers, snatched a sword from a guest, and grabbed a stick from a servant woman who was trying to bar its path. The Reverend Joseph Glanvil – who wrote about the case – came to investigate, and heard the strange noises from around the children's beds. When he went down to his horse, he found it sweating with terror, and the horse died soon afterwards.

The phantom drummer seems to have developed a voice; one morning, there was a bright light in the children's room and a voice kept shouting: "A witch, a witch!" – at least a hundred times, according to Glanvil. Mompesson woke up one night to find himself looking at a vague shape with two great staring eyes, which slowly vanished. It also developed such unpleasant habits as emptying ashes and chamberpots into the children's beds.

In 1663, William Drury was arrested at Gloucester for stealing a pig. While he was in Gloucester jail, a Wiltshire man came to see him, and Drury asked what was happening in Wiltshire. When the man said "Nothing" Drury said: "What, haven't you heard about the drumming in the house at Tedworth?" The man admitted that he had, whereupon Drury declared: "I have plagued him, and he shall never be quiet until he has made me satisfaction for taking away my drum." This, according to Glanvil, led to his being tried for a witch at Salisbury and sentenced to transportation. As soon as Drury was out of the country, peace descended on the Mompesson household. But the drummer somehow managed to escape and return to England – whereupon the disturbances began all over again. Mr Mompesson seems to have asked – by means of raps – whether Drury was responsible, and it replied in the affirmative.

How the disturbances ended is not clear – presumably they faded away, like most poltergeists. Certainly they had ceased by the time Glanvil published his account twenty years later.

Why was the clergyman Joseph Glanvil so interested in the case? Because he was in the process of writing a book called

Saducismus Triumphatus, in which he argued that witchcraft was not a mere superstition, but a genuine "occult" power. By the time his book appeared in 1681, that view was by no means popular. In England, the "witchcraft craze" had come to a sudden end in 1646 with the discrediting and death of the evil "witchfinder general" Matthew Hopkins, who was responsible for more than a hundred executions, and now most educated people dismissed the belief in witchcraft with contempt.

What is a Poltergeist?

Yet Glanvil may not have been entirely wrong. One modern investigator, Guy Lyon Playfair, spent many years in Brazil, and became interested in psychical research. When he heard of a poltergeist that was causing disturbances in a house in São Paolo, he offered his services to the Brazilian Society for Psychical Research (called the IBPP) to look into it. There

The Toby Jug restaurant in the Yorkshire village of Haworth can boast of a spectre of some distinction: poet and novelist Emily Brontë, a native of the village. According to the restaurant's owner Keith Ackroyd, Emily Brontë's ghost appears every year on December 19, the day she died. He once described for a reporter his first glimpse of the phantom in 1966 after taking over the Toby Jug. "I turned and saw this figure smiling and giggling," he said. "She walked across the room to where the stairs used to be and started to climb up to the bedroom." She was small, wore a crinoline and carried a wicker basket.

The ghost of such a famous writer might be considered an asset, but Ackroyd wanted to have it exorcized. He planned to sell the restaurant and feared that a spectre might be regarded as a liability. A curate from Leeds agreed to perform the rite, but was prevented by the Rector of Haworth who wasn't sure it was necessary. Perhaps, like many churchmen today, he takes a wary view of highly publicized exorcisms.

had been loud bangs and crashes, unexplained fires, and bedding soaked in water. Playfair witnessed many of these things, and was convinced of their genuineness. But what intrigued him was the signs that magic – or witchcraft – was somehow involved. A photograph with thread stitched through it had been found. The disturbances seemed to revolve around a girl called Nora, who had married the son of the house.

The Brazilian Society for Psychical Research tried having the house exorcised by a team of mediums. This worked for a few weeks, then the poltergeist came back. The Society then used its heaviest gun – a *candomble* specialist, or witch doctor. He performed various weird rites, and to Playfair's astonishment, the poltergeist left for good.

What surprised him was the assumption that seemed to be accepted by most Brazilians that a poltergeist can be conjured up by a witch doctor, and told to go and wreck somebody's house. But he soon realised that this view was not restricted to the uneducated masses. It was also accepted by Dr Hernani Andrade, the founder of the Brazilian Society for Psychical Research. And after a while, Playfair himself came to accept it.

Now witchcraft, which most of us regard as superstitious nonsense, is based on a belief in spirits. And this, as we have seen, is by no means an unreasonable belief. What strikes us as so strange is the idea that spirits can be persuaded to go and wreak havoc in someone's home. Yet the case of the Phantom Drummer of Tedworth suggests that William Drury possessed this power, and that he sent the "drummer" to make the life of the Mompesson family unbearable.

Was Drury a "medium"? Did he believe that the power lay in his drum, and was that why he pleaded so hard to have it returned? Unfortunately, we shall never know. Glanvil says that Drury had been a soldier under Cromwell, and had learnt magic "from some gallant books he had had of a wizard". Whatever the truth, Drury certainly obtained his revenge, for Mompesson became something of a laughing stock. Suspected of fabricating the whole story, "he suffered by it in his name, his estate and all his affairs".

The Cock Lane Ghost

The same sad fate was to overtake another household almost exactly one century later.

In November 1759, a woman named Fanny Lynes, who was lodging in the house of Richard Parsons, Clerk of St Sepulchre's Church in Smithfield, London, asked ten-year-old Elizabeth Parsons to sleep with her while her common law husband was away on business. All went well for a few nights; then the two were kept awake by scratching and rapping noises behind the wainscot. Now any modern investigator of poltergeists knows that, for some odd reason, many cases begin in this way. However, Richard Parsons had no reason to suspect that his house was haunted, and he told Fanny that it was probably the cobbler next door.

Soon afterwards, Fanny became ill with smallpox; she was six months pregnant, and her "husband" was understandably anxious. He and Fanny were unmarried only because she was his deceased wife's sister. William Kent had married Elizabeth Lynes two years earlier, but she had died in childbirth; now it looked rather as if the story were repeating itself. He moved Fanny into a house nearby, where, on 2 February 1760, she died of smallpox.

Meanwhile, the rappings in Richard Parsons' house were continuing; Parsons actually called in a carpenter to take down the wainscotting, but nothing was found. Meanwhile, the knockings got louder, and the story of the "haunted house" spread throughout the neighbourhood. They seemed to be associated with Elizabeth; they came from behind her bed, and when they were about to begin, she would begin to tremble and shiver – like Hetty Wesley in the Epworth case. Later that year, Elizabeth began to suffer from convulsions.

Like so many victims of poltergeist phenomena, Richard Parsons decided to call in a friend, the Reverend John Moore, assistant preacher at St Sepulchre's. And the Reverend Moore proceeded to communicate with the "spirit", asking it to answer his questions in the usual manner – one rap for yes, two for no. (They added a scratching noise to indicate it was displeased.)

By this means the spirit told its upsetting story. It was, it declared, the ghost of Fanny Lynes, returned from the dead to denounce her late "husband", William Kent, for killing her by poison. He had, it seemed, administered red arsenic in her "purl": a mixture of herbs and beer.

Richard Parsons was not entirely displeased to hear this story, for he was nursing a grudge against his late tenant. William Kent was a fairly rich man, having been a successful innkeeper in Norfolk, and he had lent Parsons twenty pounds, on the understanding that Parsons should repay it at a pound a month. Parsons, who seems to have been a drunkard, had failed to repay anything, possibly because he had discovered that Kent and Fanny were not married, and hoped to blackmail Kent into forgetting the loan. Kent had put the matter into the hands of his attorney.

If Parsons had been less anxious to believe the worst of his ex-tenant, he might have suspected the ghost of untruthfulness. To begin with, the knocking had begun while Fanny Lynes was still alive. And a publican named Franzen swore that he had seen a spirit in white one evening in December 1759, when Fanny had just moved from the Cock Lane house. Parsons apparently found it easier to believe that the earlier knockings had been caused by Kent's first wife Elizabeth – who was presumably also trying to denounce him for murder.

Throughout 1761, the house in Cock Lane acquired an increasing reputation for its ghosts, and the tale about Kent's supposed murders gained wide currency in the area. Kent himself heard nothing about it until January 1762, when he saw an item in the *Public Ledger* about a man who had brought a young lady from Norfolk and poisoned her in London. A few days later, another item about the Cock Lane ghost and its revelations led Kent to go along to see the Reverend John Moore. Moore, a respectable and well-liked man, could only advise Kent to attend a seance in Elizabeth's bedroom, and see for himself. Kent did this, taking with him the doctor and apothecary who had attended Fanny in her last illness. The small bedroom was crowded, and Elizabeth and her younger sister lay side by side in the bed. At first the "ghost" declined to manifest itself; but when the room had been emptied, Moore succeeded in persuading it, and they all trooped back. Now Kent listened with something like panic as he heard Moore asking the spirit if it was Kent's wife – one knock – if it had been murdered by him – one knock – and if anyone else was concerned in the murder plot – two knocks. Kent shouted indignantly, "Thou art a lying spirit!"

Now, suddenly, the ghost was famous all over London, and

Cock Lane was crowded with carriages. In February, a clergyman named Aldrich persuaded Parsons to allow his daughter to come to his vicarage in Clerkenwell to be tested. An investigating committee, including the famous Dr Johnson, was present. Inevitably, the ghost declined to manifest itself. Nor would the ghost rap on the coffin of Fanny Lynes in the vault of the church. Dr Johnson concluded it was a fraud. And this was the opinion of most of London.

On the day following this fiasco, Elizabeth was staying at the house of a comb-maker in Cow Lane when the bell of Newgate Prison began to toll – a sign that someone was to be hanged. The comb-maker asked the ghost whether someone was about to be hanged and whether it was a man or woman; the ghost answered both questions correctly. Later that day, a loose curtain began to spin on its rod – the only physical manifestation in the case.

The following day, as Elizabeth lay asleep, her father heard whispering noises; he carried a candle over to her bed, but she seemed to be asleep. The whispering continued, although the child's lips were plainly closed. In fact, the poltergeist seemed to be increasing in strength. Two nights later, the noises were so violent that their host asked them to leave. (Presumably she was sleeping away from home to avoid crowds.) Elizabeth and her father moved to the house of a Mr Missiter, near Covent Garden, and the manifestations continued, even when a maid lay in bed beside Elizabeth and held her hands and feet.

By now, the unfortunate Kent was determined to prove his innocence through the law; so the burden of proof now lay on Parsons and his daughter. Elizabeth was told that unless the ghost made itself heard that night, her father and mother would be thrown into prison. Naturally, she made sure something happened. The servants peered through a crack in the door, and saw her take a piece of board and hide it in the bed. Later, when there were people in the room, the knocking noises sounded from the bed. In fact, the listeners noticed that the knocks were coming from the bed and not, as usual, from around the room. The bed was searched and the board found. And the next day, the newspapers published the story of the "fraud".

On 25 February 1762, there appeared a pamphlet entitled: *The Mystery Revealed; Containing a Series of Transactions and Authentic Testimonials respecting the supposed Cock Lane Ghost, which have been concealed from the Public* – the author was probably Johnson's friend Oliver Goldsmith. A satirical play

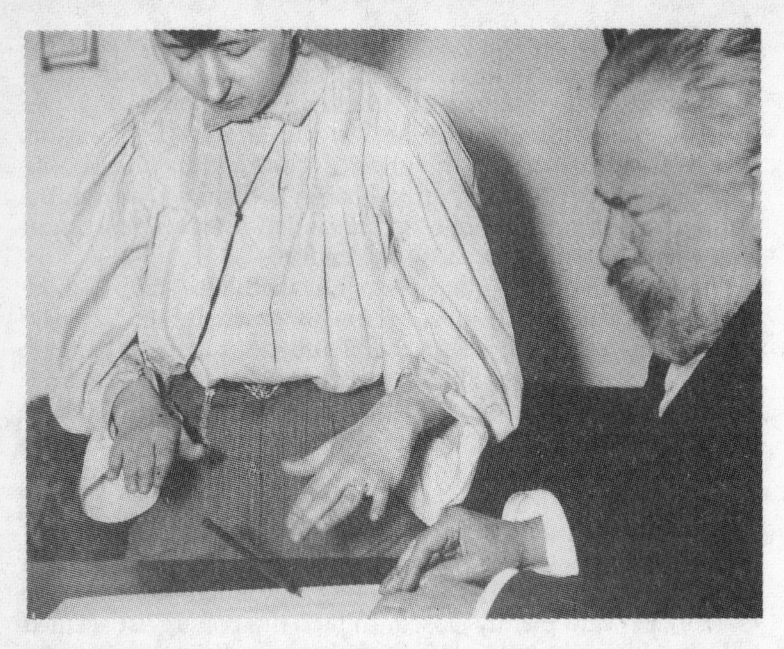

Unexplained talents, levitation by Stanislawa Tomczyk

called *The Drummer or the Haunted House* was presented at Covent Garden. And William Kent began legal proceedings against Richard Parsons. In July 1762, Mr and Mrs Parsons, and a woman called Mary Frazer – who had often acted as "questioner" to the ghost – appeared before magistrates in the Guildhall. Parsons was charged with trying to take away the life of William Kent by charging him with murder. The judges remained unconvinced by the evidence of neighbours who had heard raps resounding from all over the room, and who were certain that Elizabeth could not have made them. And finally, Parsons was sentenced to two years in prison, and to stand three times in the pillory; his wife was sentenced to one year, and Mary Frazer to six months. The Reverend Moore and one of his associates had to pay out £588 in damages to Kent. There was universal sympathy for Parsons, and when he stood in the pillory, the mob took up a collection for him – an unusual gesture for a period when malefactors were often badly injured in the pillory. (Later in the year a man convicted of sodomy was stoned to death in the same pillory.)

For more than two centuries, the Cock Lane ghost became a synonym for an imposture. When Andrew Lang wrote about it in 1894, he began his chapter: "If one phantom is more discredited than another, it is the Cock Lane ghost." Yet for anyone studying the case today, this view seems absurd. Nothing could be more obvious than that the Cock Lane ghost was a poltergeist like the hundreds of others that have been recorded down the ages. Unfortunately, it is now too late for us to discover certain essential facts that might help to explain it. For example, what kind of a girl *was* Elizabeth Parsons? She was rather younger than most poltergeist-children, but she may well have been sexually mature for her age. If her father was something of a drunkard and a spendthrift – as the records indicate – then it seems fairly certain that the Parsons household was not a happy one. The father of Christine Beauchamp – Morton Prince's famous case of multiple personality – was a similar type of person, and his daughter had severe psychological problems as a consequence. We know that Christine Beauchamp became fixated on her father's closest friend William Jones, and transferred to him all her adoration. It is conceivable that Elizabeth Parsons felt the same about William Kent. In which case, sleeping in his bed while he was away must have aroused morbid emotions – especially if she was aware that Kent and Fanny were "living in sin". The convulsions that began a year after the disturbances certainly suggest she was passing through a period of emotional upheaval. But since we know so little about Elizabeth, all these things must remain a matter for speculation.

Only one thing seems fairly certain: that the spirit itself was neither that of Elizabeth Kent nor of Fanny Lynes; it was the usual mischievous poltergeist, bent on creating as much havoc and confusion as possible. It seems to confirm G.K. Chesterton's remark that the only definite thing that can be said about such spirits is that they tell lies.

The Seeress of Prevorst

The Phantom Drummer of Tedworth and the Cock Lane Ghost demonstrate that the "Age of Reason" did not take kindly to ghosts. Dr Johnson, who was sure the Cock Lane ghost was a fraud, died in 1784, and his death signalled the end of an era. Not long after that, everything changed. Romanticism had arrived, and quite suddenly, everybody wanted to read about ghosts and haunted castles and vampires.

But all that, of course, was mere fiction. That is why, in 1828, a German book about real ghosts became an instant bestseller. It was called *The Seeress of Prevorst*, and was written by a rich and eccentric doctor called Justinus Kerner, who practised in Weinberg, near Heilbronn. In 1826, he was consulted by the relatives of a "haunted" woman called Friederike Hauffe, who was dying of a wasting disease. She had lost all her teeth and looked like a walking skeleton.

It seemed that marriage was responsible for her sad condition. Ever since childhood she had fallen into trances, seen visions, and conversed with invisible spirits. She could also accurately predict the future. When she was nineteen, she had married a cousin, and gone into depression; at twenty, her first child was born, and she began to develop hysterical symptoms. Every evening, she fell into a trance in which she saw spirits of the dead.

Kerner was at first inclined to be sceptical about her visions and spirits – he put them down to hysteria. Yet he found Friederike Hauffe a fascinating case for study. She claimed to be able to see into the human body, and certainly had a remarkably precise knowledge of the nervous system. She could read with her stomach – Kerner tested her by making her lie down with her eyes closed, and laid documents on her bare midriff; she read them perfectly. She could make geometrical drawings at great speed, even in the dark, and could draw perfect circles that looked as if they had been drawn by compasses. She claimed that her spirit often left her body and hovered above it.

Kerner tried ordinary medicines on her, but they had no effect. Friederike told him that if he placed her in a "magnetic trance" the spirits would instruct him on how to treat her, but he was reluctant to accept this advice. Eventually, he decided that he might as well try the effects of mesmerism.

Friederike reacted well to "magnetism", passing easily into a trance. But Kerner remained sceptical about the things she said in this condition. Then, one day, a remarkable experience changed his mind. Friederike declared that she was being haunted by an unpleasant man with a squint. From her description, Kerner recognised him as a man who had died a few years earlier. It seemed, according to Friederike, that the man was suffering from a guilty conscience. He had been involved in embezzlement and, after his death, another man had been blamed. Now he wanted to clear the man's name, for the sake of his widow. This could be done by means of a certain document, which would be found in a chest. The spirit "showed" Friederike the room where the document was to be found, and a man who was working there. Her description was so good that Kerner was able to identify him as a certain Judge Heyd. In her "vision", Friederike had seen Judge Heyd sitting in a certain place in this room, and the chest containing the document on the table. The document was apparently not in its proper numerical order, which is why it had not been found.

When Kerner told him about his patient's vision, Judge Heyd was astounded; he *had* been sitting in the position described on that particular day (Christmas Day), and the chest, contrary to regulations, had been left open on the table. When they searched, the document turned up where Friederike had said it would. The widow of the man who had been wrongly accused was able to obtain redress.

From now on, Kerner believed in Friederike's supernatural powers, and took whatever she said seriously. She told him that we are surrounded by spirits all the time, and that she was able to see them. These spirits often try to attract our attention in various ways: knocking, movement of objects, throwing of sand. And by way of convincing him, Friederike persuaded one of the spirits to make rapping noises, to make gravel and ash fall from the air, and to make a stool float up into the air. Kerner watched with amazement as the stool rose gently, then floated down again.

Friederike provided him with further proof of the accuracy of her visions when she succeeded in putting an end to a haunting. Kerner heard about a house where the ghost of an old man was frightening the inhabitants. He brought one of them, a woman, along to see Friederike; the seeress went into a trance and explained that the ghost was that of a man called Bellon, who was an "earthbound spirit" as a result of defrauding two orphans. Kerner made enquiries, but no one had ever heard of a man called Bellon. But since the ghost claimed that he had been Burgomeister, it seemed probable that some record existed. He claimed he had been Burgomeister in the year 1700, and had died at the age of seventy-nine. Armed with this information,

Kerner asked the present mayor to check the legal documents; they soon found that in the year 1700, a man called Bellon *had* been Burgomeister and director of the local orphanage. He had died in 1740 at the age of seventy-nine. After "confessing", the spirit took its departure.

While Friederike was in Kerner's house, there were constant poltergeist phenomena: knocks and raps, noises like the rattling of chains, gravel thrown through the window, and a knitting needle that flew through the air and landed in a glass of water. When Friederike was visited by a spirit one night her sister heard her say, "Open it yourself", then saw a book on the table open itself. A poltergeist tugged her boots off her feet as she lay on the bed, and threw a lampshade across the room. In the Kerners' bedroom, a table was thrown across the room. The poltergeist threw a stool at a maidservant who went into Friederike's room while she lay asleep. It extinguished a night-light and made a candle glow.

Friederike also produced what would later be called "spirit teachings", an amazingly complex system of philosophy in which man is described as consisting of body, soul and spirit, and of being surrounded by a nerve aura which carries on the vital processes. She spoke about various cycles in human existence – life cycles (or circles) and sun cycles, corresponding to various spiritual conditions. She also described a remarkable universal language from ancient times, said to be "the language of the inner life". (A mystical sect was founded to expound those doctrines after her death.)

All these mediumistic activities made Friederike more and more feeble, and she died in 1829 at the age of twenty-eight. Kerner's book *The Seeress of Prevorst* (the name of the Swabian village where she was born) created a sensation.

In the second half of the nineteenth century, as the scientific reaction against spiritualism increased, *The Seeress of Prevorst* ceased to be taken seriously by those engaged in psychical research, and by the twentieth century it had been virtually forgotten. Writing about it in his *Modern Spiritualism* (1902), the sceptical Frank Podmore – who believed that all poltergeists are due to naughty children – dismissed most of the evidence as second-hand, while another eminent researcher, E.J. Dingwall (writing in *Abnormal Hypnotic Phenomena*) seems to feel that Kerner was stupid to take her claims seriously, and that if he had remained sceptical and treated her simply as a case of hysteria, she would have lived longer. But reading Kerner's own account, it is difficult to see how he would have remained sceptical without being downright dishonest or blind; on one occasion, he saw a cloudy figure hovering in front of her, and although it had vanished when he came back with a lamp, Friederike continued to stare at the spot as though listening to it.

In fact, we can see that the case of the seeress of Prevorst is a thoroughly typical case of poltergeist phenomena caused by a medium. In detail after detail, it sounds like any number of other cases of "haunting". If anyone killed Friederike Hauffe, it was the spirits themselves, who must have been using her energy to manifest themselves. No doubt the poltergeist phenomena were unspectacular because Friederike was weak from the moment Kerner set eyes on her. (In a case cited by the novelist William de Morgan, a maidservant who was able to cause rapping noises gradually lost her powers as she became weaker from tuberculosis.)

In another of his books, Kerner describes another remarkable case with some of the characteristics of poltergeist haunting. He was asked to treat a "possessed" peasant girl in Orlach, near Stuttgart. For some reason which is not clear, she was persecuted by "spirits" from the age of twenty, and there were the usual bangs and crashes, movements of furniture, and even outbreaks of fire. Then, after five months of this, she saw two ghosts, one of a nun dressed in white, the other of a monk dressed in black. The nun asserted that she had been smuggled into the monastery disguised as a cook, and had had two children by the black monk, both of whom he had killed at birth. He also murdered three monks during the four-year period she was with him; and, when he suspected she was about to betray him, he killed her too. The black monk also spoke to the possessed girl, saying that he was the son of a nobleman from nearby Geislingen, and that as the Superior at the monastery of Orlach, he had seduced a number of nuns and killed the children they bore. He also confessed to killing monks. The bodies, he said, he threw into a hole in a wall.

The white nun told the girl that her sufferings would cease only if her parents agreed to their cottage's demolition. By this time they were so desperate that they agreed. On 5 March 1833 the house was finally demolished. Most of the walls were made of mud, but one corner was constructed of limestone, obviously part of a far older building. When this was pulled down, they found underneath it an empty well containing a number of human bones, including those of children. The girl's possession ceased from the moment the wall collapsed.

The story sounds like a typical invention of a German romantic novelist; but Kerner devotes a whole book to it, describing it in the same detail as his investigation of Friederike Hauffe. In spite of this, modern investigators are inclined not to take it seriously. Yet readers who are impressed by the clarity and detail of Kerner's reporting may feel that this case of the possessed girl of Orlach is one of the most convincing arguments for the close connection between poltergeists and spirits of the dead.

Ten years after publication of *The Seeress of Prevorst*, another doctor – this time of philosophy – produced an equally remarkable account of a case of possession, this time benevolent. In *Die Schutzgeister* (*The Guardian Spirit*, 1839), Heinrich Werner identifies his eighteen-year-old subject only as "R.O.". Like Friederike, she had been subject to all kinds of illnesses, then, at a certain point, found herself haunted by spirits. One day the girl fell into a trance; and from then on she was able to do so at will, and to supply Werner with all kinds of information obtained "clairvoyantly". She had a guardian spirit called Albert, who seems to have acted rather like the "spirit guide" of later mediums. And the spirit who caused her so much trouble was – again – a wicked monk. One day, when the girl claimed that the wicked monk was present in the room, Werner was puzzled to hear an odd sound coming from a small table – like a cup rattling on a saucer. This occurred a number of times, becoming steadily louder (a typical characteristic of poltergeist noises); R.O. said that the monk was producing the noise, and was delighted at Werner's astonishment – which also sounds typical of a poltergeist.

One day, Werner was startled to hear a loud crash from an empty room; he rushed in to find that two large flowerpots, which had stood on the window sill, had been hurled to the floor so violently that there was earth all over the room. The blind was closed and there was no breeze. One of the curtains had also been twisted around a birdcage. Later that day, Werner went to call on R.O., who went into a trance, and then told Werner that the black monk had been responsible for smashing the flowerpots (Werner had not mentioned this to her). Albert, apparently, had ejected him from the house.

Werner was greatly impressed by his patient's clairvoyant powers. She demonstrated these one day when she woke up from a trance and told him that she had seen herself driving in a green-lacquered chaise. Now Werner had, at the time, made some enquiries about a chaise that was for sale in a town some fifteen hours away, and he expected to get an answer in about a week. R.O. told him he would hear much sooner than that – in fact, the following afternoon; she also went on to describe the chaise, in some detail. The following afternoon, Werner received a message about the chaise, and discovered that the girl was right in every detail.

Her most dramatic piece of clairvoyance concerned her younger sister. One day, in a trance, she cried out: "Albert, help me! Emilie is falling down into the street." Then, after a short period, she said: "Thank God, help has already come!"

Asked what had happened, she explained that her little sister had been leaning out of a top-storey window, trying to grab a rope suspended from a winch above the window; she had been on the point of falling when her father had entered the room and pulled her back.

Werner contacted the father to ask if anything remarkable had happened on that particular day, and received a reply which Werner printed in his book. It said that the father had been sitting in his office when he had felt uneasy. He went home, and went upstairs, in time to find his daughter had leaned too far out of the window to catch the rope, and could not get back into the room; he grabbed her dress and hauled her back in. R.O. said that it was Albert, the guardian spirit, who had made her father feel uneasy.

The Haunting of Willington Mill

The cases described by Justinus Kerner and Heinrich Werner caused widespread interest all over Europe. A lady novelist named Mrs Catherine Crowe was so impressed by *The Seeress of Prevorst* that she decided to translate it into English. And after her translation had appeared in 1845, she went on and wrote her own bestseller, *The Nightside of Nature,* which was still selling on railway bookstalls at the end of the century. She collected stories about ghosts, poltergeists, premonitions of the future and haunted houses.

The following extract from her book will demonstrate why it remained a bestseller for more than half a century.

> But, perhaps, one of the most remarkable cases of haunting in modern times, is that of Willington, near Newcastle, in my account of which, however, I find myself anticipated by Mr Howitt; and as he has had the advantage of visiting the place, which I have not, I shall take the liberty of borrowing his description of it, prefacing the account with the following letter from Mr Procter, the owner of the house, who, it will be seen, vouches for the general authenticity of the narrative. The letter was written in answer to one from me, requesting some more precise information than I had been able to obtain.
>
> "Josh. Proctor hopes C. Crowe will excuse her note having remained two weeks unanswered, during which time, J.P. has been from home, or particularly engaged. Feeling averse to add to the publicity the circumstances occurring in his house, at Willington, have already obtained, J.P. would rather not furnish additional particulars; but if C.C. is not in possession of the number of *Howitt's Journal*, which contains a variety of details on the subject, he will be glad to forward her one. He would at the same time, assure C. Crowe of the strict accuracy of that portion of W. Howitt's narrative which is extracted from *Richardson's Table Book*. W. Howitt's statements derived from his recollection of verbal communications with branches of J. Procter's family, are likewise essentially correct, though, as might be expected in some degree, erroneous circumstantially.
>
> "J.P. takes leave to express his conviction, that the unbelief of the educated classes, in apparitions of the deceased, and kindred phenomena, is not grounded on a fair philosophic examination of the facts which have induced the popular belief of all ages and countries; and that it will be found, by succeeding ages, to have been nothing better than unreasoning and unreasonable prejudice.
>
> ["Willington, near Newcastle-on-Tyne,
> 7th mo. 22, 1847."]

"VISITS TO REMARKABLE PLACES.
BY WILLIAM HOWITT.
THE HAUNTED HOUSE AT WILLINGTON, NEAR NEWCASTLE-ON-TYNE.

"We have of late years settled it as an established fact, that ghosts and haunted houses were the empty creation of ignorant times. We have comfortably persuaded ourselves that such fancies only hovered in the twilight of superstition, and that in these enlightened days they had vanished for ever. How often has it been triumphantly referred to, as a proof that all such things were the offspring of ignorance – that nothing of the kind is heard of now? What shall we say, then, to the following facts? Here we have ghosts and a haunted house still. We have them in the face of our vaunted noon-day light, in the midst of a busy and a populous neighbourhood, in the neighbourhood of a large and most intelligent town, and in a family neither ignorant, nor in any other respect superstitious. For years have these ghosts and hauntings disturbed the quiet of a highly respectable family, and continue to haunt and disturb, spite of the incredulity of the wise, the investigations of the curious, and the anxious vigilance of the suffering family itself.

"Between the railway running from Newcastle-on-Tyne to North Shields, and the river Tyne, there lie in a hollow some few cottages, a parsonage, and a mill and a miller's house. These constitute the hamlet of Willington. Just above these the railway is carried across the valley on lofty arches, and from it you look down on the mill and cottages, lying at a considerable depth below. The mill is a large steam flour mill, like a factory, and the miller's house stands near it, but not adjoining it. None of the cottages which lie between these premises and the railway, either, are in contact with them. The house stands on a sort of little promontory, round which runs the channel of a water-course, which appears to fill and empty with the tides. On one side of the mill and house, slopes away, upwards, a field, to a considerable distance, where it is terminated by other enclosures; on the other stands a considerable extent of ballast-hill, ie, one of the numerous hills on the banks of the Tyne, made by the deposit of ballast from the vessels trading thither. At a distance the top of the mill seems about level with the country around it. The place lies about half-way between Newcastle and North Shields.

"This mill is, I believe, the property of, and is worked by, Messrs. Unthank and Procter. Mr Joseph Procter resides on the spot in the house just by the mill, as already stated. He is a member of the Society of Friends, a gentleman in the very prime of life; and his wife, an intelligent lady, is of a family of Friends in Carlisle. They have several young children. This very respectable and well-informed family, belonging to a sect which of all others is most accustomed to control, to regulate, and to put down even the imagination – the last people in the world, as it would appear, in fact, to be affected by any mere imaginary terrors or impressions, have for years been persecuted by the most extraordinary noises and apparitions.

"The house is not an old house, as will appear; it was built about the year 1800. It has no particularly spectral look about it. Seeing it in passing, or within, ignorant of its real character, one should by no means say that it was a place likely to have the reputation of being haunted. Yet looking down from the railway, and seeing it and the mill lying in a deep hole, one might imagine various strange noises likely to be heard in such a place in the night, from vessels on the river, from winds sweeping and howling down the gully in which it stands, from engines in the neighbourhood connected with coal mines, one of which, I could not tell where, was making, at the time I was there, a wild sighing noise, as I stood on the hill above. There is not any passage, however, known of under the house, by which subterraneous noises could be heard, nor are they merely noises that are heard; distinct apparitions are declared to be seen.

"Spite of the unwillingness of Mr Procter that these mysterious circumstances should become quite public, and averse as he is to make known himself these strange visitations, they were of such a nature that they soon became rumoured over the whole neighbourhood. Numbers of people hurried to the place to inquire into the truth of them, and at length a remarkable occurrence brought them into print. What this occurrence was, the pamphlet which appeared, and which was afterwards reprinted in *The Local Historian's Table-book,* published by Mr M.A. Richardson, of Newcastle, and which I here copy, will explain. It will be seen that the writer of this article has the fullest faith in the reality of what he relates, as indeed vast numbers of the best-informed inhabitants of the neighbourhood have.

"AUTHENTIC ACCOUNT OF A VISIT TO THE HAUNTED HOUSE AT WILLINGTON.

"Were we to draw an inference from the number of cases of reported visitations from the invisible world that have been made public of late, we might be led to imagine that the days of supernatural agency were about to recommence, and that ghosts and hobgoblins were about to resume their sway over the fears of mankind. Did we, however, indulge such an apprehension, a glance at the current tone of the literature and philosophy of the day, when treating of these subjects, would show a measure of unbelief regarding them as scornful and uncompromising as the veriest atheist or materialist could desire. Notwithstanding the prevalence of this feeling amongst the educated classes, there is a curiosity and interest manifested in every occurrence of this nature, that indicates a lurking faith at bottom, which an affected scepticism fails entirely to conceal. We feel, therefore, that we need not apologise to our readers for introducing the following particulars of a *visit* to a house in this immediate neighbourhood, which had become notorious for some years previous, as being 'haunted'; and several of the reputed deeds, or misdeeds, of its supernatural visitant had been published far and wide by rumour's thousand tongues. We deem it as worthy to be chronicled as the doings of its contemporary *genii* at Windsor, Dublin, Liverpool, Carlisle, and Sunderland, and which have all likewise hitherto failed, after public investigation, to receive a solution consistent with a rejection of spiritual agency.

"We have visited the house in question, which is well known to many of our readers as being near a large steam corn-mill, in full view of Willington viaduct, on the Newcastle and Shields Railway; and it may not be irrelevant to mention that it is quite detached from the mill, or any other premises, and has no cellaring under it. The proprietor of the house, who lives in it, declines to make public the particulars of the disturbance to which he has been subjected, and it must be understood that the account of the visit we are about to lay before our readers is derived from a friend to whom Mr Drury presented a copy of his correspondence on the subject, with power to make such use of it as he thought proper. We learned that the house had been reputed, at least one room in it, to have been haunted forty years ago, and had afterwards been undisturbed for a long period, during some years of which quietude the present occupant lived in it unmolested. We are also informed, that about the time that the premises were building, viz, in 1800 or 1801, there were reports of some deed of darkness having been committed by someone employed about them. We should extend this account beyond the limits we have set to ourselves, did we now enter upon a full account of the strange things which have been seen and heard about the place by several of the neighbours, as well as those which are reported to have been seen, heard, and felt by the inmates, whose servants have been changed on that account many times. We proceed, therefore, to give the following letters, which have been passed between individuals of undoubted veracity; leaving the reader to draw his own conclusions on the subject.

"(Copy, No. 1.)

"To Mr Procter, 17th June, 1840.

"Sir, – Having heard from indisputable authority, viz, that of my excellent friend, Mr Davison, of Low Willington, farmer, that you and your family are disturbed by most unaccountable noises at night, I beg leave to tell you that I have read attentively Wesley's account of such things, but with, I must confess, no great belief; but an account of this report coming from one of your sect, which I admire for candour and simplicity, my curiosity is excited to a high pitch, which I would fain satisfy. My desire is to remain alone in the house all night, with no companion but my own watch-dog, in which, as far as courage and fidelity are concerned, I place much more reliance than upon any three young gentlemen I know of. And it is also my hope, that if I have a fair trial, I shall be able to unravel this mystery. Mr Davison will give you every satisfaction if you take the trouble to inquire of him concerning me.

"I am, Sir,

"Yours most respectfully,

"EDWARD DRURY

"At C.C. Embleton's, Surgeon,

"No. 10, Church-street, Sunderland.

"(COPY, No. 2.)

"Joseph Procter's respects to Edward Drury, whose note he received a few days ago, expressing a wish to pass a night in his house at Willington. As the family is going from home on the 23rd instant, and one of Unthank and Procter's men will sleep in the house, if E.D. feels inclined to come, on or after the 24th, to spend a night in it, he is at liberty so to do, with or without his faithful dog, which, by the bye, can be of no possible use, except as company. At the same time, J.P. thinks it best to inform him, that particular disturbances are far from frequent at present, being only occasional, and quite uncertain, and therefore the satisfaction of E.D.'s curiosity must be considered as problematical. The best chance will be afforded by his sitting up alone in the third story till it be fairly daylight, say two or three a.m.

"Willington, 6th mo. 21st, 1840.

"J.P. will leave word with T. Maun, foreman, to admit E.D.

"Mr Procter left home with his family on the 23rd

June, and got an old servant, who was then out of place in consequence of ill-health, to take charge of the house during their absence. Mr P. returned alone, on account of business, on the 3rd of July, on the evening of which day Mr Drury and his companion also unexpectedly arrived. After the house had been locked up, every corner of it was minutely examined. The room out of which the apparition issued is too shallow to contain any person. Mr Drury and his friend had lights by them, and were satisfied that there was no one in the house besides Mr P., the servant, and themselves.

"(Copy, No. 3.)

"Monday Morning, July 6, 1840.

"To Mr Procter,

"Dear Sir, – I am sorry I was not at home to receive you yesterday, when you kindly called to inquire for me. I am happy to state that I am really surprised that I have been so little affected as I am, after that horrid and most awful affair. The only bad effect that I feel is a heavy dulness in one of my ears – the right one. I call it a heavy dulness, because I not only do not hear distinctly, but feel in it a constant noise. This I never was affected with before; but I doubt not it will go off. I am persuaded that no one went to your house at any time more *disbelieving in respect to seeing anything peculiar*; now no one can be more satisfied than myself. I will, in the course of a few days, send you a full detail of all I saw and heard. Mr Spence and two other gentlemen came down to my house in the afternoon, to hear my detail; but, sir, could I account for these noises from natural causes, yet, so firmly am I persuaded of the horrid apparition, that I would affirm that what I saw with my eyes was a punishment to me for my scoffing and unbelief; that I am assured that, as far as the horror is concerned, they are happy that believe and have not seen. Let me trouble you, sir, to give me the address of your sister, from Cumberland, who was alarmed, and also of your brother. I would feel a satisfaction in having a line from them; and, above all things, it will be a great cause of joy to me, if you never allow your young family to be in that horrid house again. Hoping you will write a few lines at your leisure,

"I remain, dear Sir,
"Yours very truly,
"EDWARD DRURY.

"(COPY, No. 4.)
"Willington, 7th mo. 9, 1840.

"Respected Friend, E. Drury,

"Having been at Sunderland, I did not receive thine of the 6th till yesterday morning. I am glad to hear thou art getting well over the effects of thy unlooked-for visitation. I hold in respect thy bold and manly assertion of the truth in the face of that ridicule and ignorant conceit with which that which is called the supernatural, in the present day, is usually assailed.

"I shall be glad to receive thy detail, in which it will be needful to be very particular in showing that thou couldst not be asleep, or attacked by nightmare, or mistake a reflection of the candle, as some sagaciously suppose.

"I remain, respectfully,
"Thy friend,
"JOSH. PROCTER.

"P.S. – I have about thirty witnesses to various things which cannot be satisfactorily accounted for on any other principle than that of spiritual agency.

"(COPY, No. 5.)
"Sunderland, July 13, 1840.

"DEAR SIR, – I hereby, according to promise in my last letter, forward you a true account of what I heard and saw at your house, in which I was led to pass the night from various rumours circulated by most respectable parties, particularly from an account by my esteemed friend Mr Davison, whose name I mentioned to you in a former letter. Having received your sanction to visit your mysterious dwelling, I went, on the 3rd of July, accompanied by a friend of mine, T. Hudson. This was not according to promise, nor in accordance with my first intent, as I wrote you I would come alone; but I felt gratified at your kindness in not alluding to the liberty I had taken, as it ultimately proved for the best. I must here mention that, not expecting you at home, I had in my pocket a brace of pistols, determining in my mind to let one of them drop before the miller, as if by accident, for fear he should presume to play tricks upon me; but after my interview with you, I felt there was no occasion for weapons, and did not load them, after you had allowed us to inspect as minutely as we pleased every portion of the house. I sat down on the third story landing, fully expecting to account for any noises that I might hear, in a philosophical manner. This was about eleven o'clock p.m. About ten minutes to twelve we both heard a noise, as if a number of people were pattering with their bare feet upon the floor; and yet, so singular was the noise, that I could not minutely determine from whence it proceeded. A few minutes afterwards we heard a noise, as if some one was knocking with his knuckles among our feet; this was followed by a hollow cough from the very room from which the apparition proceeded. The only noise after this, was as if a person was rustling against the wall in coming up stairs. At a quarter to one, I told my friend that, feeling a little cold, I would like to go to bed, as we might hear the noise equally well there; he replied, that he would not go to bed till daylight. I took up a note which I had accidentally dropped, and began to read it, after which I took out my watch to ascertain the time, and found that it wanted ten minutes to one. In taking my eyes from the watch they became rivetted upon a closet door, which I distinctly saw open, and saw also the figure of a female attired in greyish garments, with the head inclining downwards, and one hand pressed upon the chest, as if in pain, and the other, viz, the right hand, extended towards the floor, with the index finger pointing downwards. It advanced with an apparently cautious step across the floor towards me; immediately as it approached my friend, who was slumbering, its right hand was extended towards him; I then rushed at it, giving, as Mr Procter states, a most awful yell; but, instead of grasping it, I fell upon my friend, and I recollected nothing distinctly for nearly three hours afterwards. I have since learnt that I was carried down stairs in an agony of fear and terror.

"I hereby certify that the above account is strictly true and correct in every respect.

"North Shields. EDWARD DRURY.

Mrs Crowe not only publishes the full correspondence between Dr Drury and Joseph Procter, but an account by a local historian, another by the owner of a local journal, and descriptions by four other people who had seen the ghost. In fact, there seemed to be more than one; there was also a man in a surplice who glided across a second-floor room at a distance of a few feet from the floor. The local historian adds to his account the information that Mr Procter has recently discovered an old book that states that similar hauntings had taken place in an older house that had been built on the same spot two hundred years before. Mrs Crowe ends her account by mentioning that Mr Procter has now decided to leave the house, and turn it into "small tenements" for his workpeople.

• chapter seven •

SOME TRANSATLANTIC CASES

The Phelps Case

The evil spirit in *The Exorcist* is apparently conjured up by a child playing with an ouija board. This is by no means as far-fetched as it sounds. It was an interest in ghosts that disrupted the home of the Rev. Eliakim Phelps in 1850.

The Reverend Phelps lived in Stratford, Connecticut, and had married a widow with four children. He was interested in clairvoyance, and attempted to treat illnesses by means of mesmerism. He was understandably excited by the news of the strange events at the home of the Fox family in 1849. And in March 1850, when he entertained a visitor from New York, the two of them arranged some kind of amateur seance, which was not particularly successful, although they managed to obtain a few raps.

A few days later, on Sunday March 10, the family returned from church to find the front door wide open and the place in disorder. Their first assumption was that they had been burgled; but inspection showed that nothing had been taken, and a gold watch left on a table was untouched. That afternoon, the family went off to church again, but this time the Reverend Phelps stayed behind to keep watch. He may well have dozed; at all events, nothing disturbed him. But when the family returned from church, the place again showed signs of an intruder. Furniture was scattered, and in the main bedroom, a nightgown and chemise had been laid out on the bed, with the arms folded across the breast, and a pair of stockings placed to make it look like a corpse laid out for burial. In another room, clothing and cushions had been used to make various dummies, which were arranged in a tableau, "in attitudes of extreme devotion, some with their foreheads nearly touching the floor", and with open Bibles in front of them. Clearly, the poltergeist had a sense of ironic humour.

From then on, the Phelps poltergeist practised its skill as a designer of tableaux. The astonishing thing was that these were done so quickly. One observer, a Dr Webster, remarked that it would have taken half a dozen women several hours to construct the "dummies" that the poltergeist made within minutes. One figure was so life-like that when the three-year-old boy went into the room, he thought his mother was kneeling in prayer, and whispered "Be still . . ."

That it *was* a poltergeist became clear the following day, when objects began to fly through the air. A bucket flew downstairs, an umbrella leapt through the air, and spoons, bits of tin and keys were thrown around. A candlestick jumped off the mantelpiece, then beat the floor violently until it broke. There were loud pounding noises as if someone was trying to demolish the house with an axe, and loud screams.

The poltergeist probably derived its strength from the fact that it had two "focuses" in the house – Harry, aged twelve, and Anna, who was sixteen. Harry was persecuted by the "spirit". When he went for a drive in the carriage with his stepfather, twenty stones were flung into the carriage. On one occasion he was snatched up into the air so that his head nearly struck the ceiling; he was thrown into a cistern of water, and tied up and suspended from a tree. In front of a visiting clergyman, the legs of his trousers were violently torn open from the bottom to above the knee.

After this, the poltergeist started to break glass; it smashed seventy-one window panes and various glass articles. Another of its favourite tricks was to write on sheets of paper; when the Reverend Phelps turned his back on his writing table, he heard the scratching of the pen, and found written on the paper: "Very nice paper and nice ink for the devil." (Typically, poltergeists seem to object to being watched while they do things like this; they wait until no one is looking.)

Phelps tried communicating with the "spirit" by means of

raps, and found that it would answer his questions. There seemed to be more than one spirit present; but the author of most of the mischief seemed to be a French clerk, who had handled a settlement for Mrs Phelps, and who had since died; he now claimed to be in hell because he had cheated Mrs Phelps. Her husband investigated this claim, and found that there *had* been a minor fraud; but it had hardly been as serious as the "spirit" seemed to believe. On another occasion the raps told Phelps to put his hand under the table; when he did this his hand was grasped by another hand, warm and human.

A well-known psychic named Andrew Jackson Davis visited the Phelps home, and put forward a theory very similar to that of Mrs Crowe. He said that the phenomena were caused by "magnetism" and by "electricity": the magnetism attracting objects towards the boy and girl, the electricity causing them to fly in the opposite direction. But Davis – the author of a bestselling work of "spirit dictation" called *The Principles of Nature* – also agreed that there were spirits present – he claimed to have seen five of them.

The poltergeist – or poltergeists – became increasingly destructive. Pieces of paper burst into flame, although always where they could be seen; sometimes, the ashes of burnt papers were found in drawers. All kinds of objects were smashed – Phelps estimated that the poltergeist had done about two hundred dollars' worth of damage. And the poltergeist also attacked the eldest girl, Anna. A reporter was sitting with the mother and daughter when the girl shouted that someone had pinched her; they rolled up her sleeve and found a severe fresh pinch mark on her arm. On another occasion, there was a loud smacking noise, and a red mark appeared on her face.

In October 1851, more than a year after the disturbances began, the mother and children went off to Pennsylvania and stayed there until the following spring. The poltergeist did not follow them; and when they returned to Stratford, nothing more happened.

It seems fairly clear that the Reverend Phelps made a mistake in attracting the attention of spirits to his home by holding the seance; they discovered that there were two excellent mediums in the house, and the result was one of the most spectacular cases of poltergeist disturbance on record. The assertion by one of the "spirits" that he was a French clerk, now in hell, need not be taken too seriously; another observer, the Reverend John Mitchell, also communicated with the "spirits" by means of raps, and received insulting replies in bad language. The Phelps poltergeists seem to have been the usual crowd of invisible juvenile delinquents.

The Dagg Poltergeist

It is rare for poltergeists to talk, but the "spirit" that haunted the farm of the Dagg family is a fascinating exception. The following account is from a book called *Ghosts and Poltergeists* by a Catholic priest, Father Herbert Thurston.

On 15 September 1889, the family of George Dagg, a farmer living in the township of Clarendon, Province of Quebec, began, we are told, to be troubled by some strange spirit of mischief which played havoc with their peaceful home and drove them to distraction. The family consisted of George Dagg, aged thirty-five years, his wife Susan, little Mary Dagg aged four, little

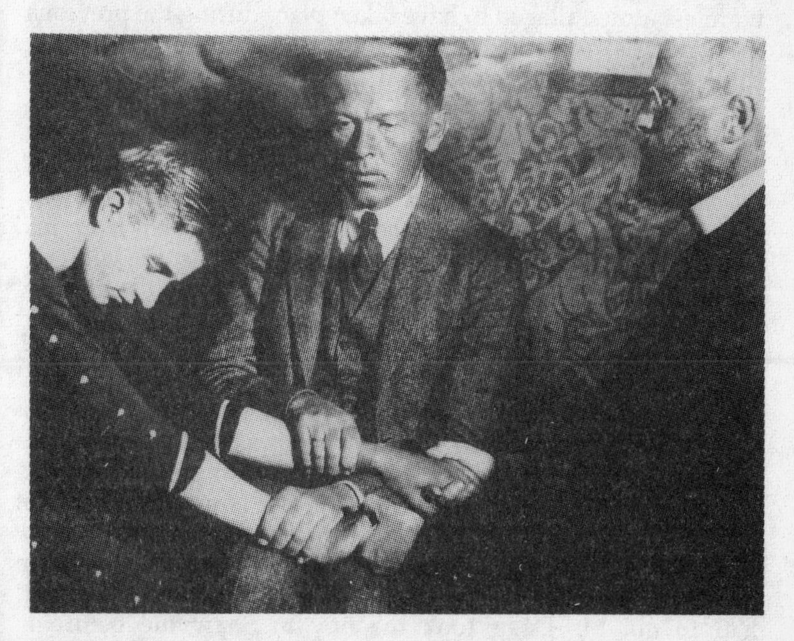

Willi Schneider, is tightly controlled during a seance, 1921

Johnny Dagg aged two, and Dinah Burden McLean aged eleven. This little girl Dinah, an orphan, was sent out from Scotland by Mr Quartier, and had been adopted from the Belleville Home by Mr Dagg five years earlier. Previously to the commencement of these troubles, she was a stout, rosy-cheeked Scotch girl. "Now," says the report, "her cheeks are sunken in, dark rings encircle her eyes, and she is a mere shadow of her former self." As constantly happens in such cases, the farmer folk of the surrounding country believed that some sort of witchcraft or magic must be at the bottom of the troubles, and a certain Mrs Wallace and her children fell under suspicion. The one fact which was a matter of observation was that when Dinah was away from the house the disturbances ceased.

The account of the case, which was printed in *The Recorder* of Brockville, Canada, was furnished by a certain Mr Woodcock, described as an artist well known in the Dominion, who had also lived in New York and in Paris. He visited the Daggs on Friday, 15 November, and spent most of his time with them until the Sunday evening. During these three days he made notes of what he could learn from the family and the neighbours, and seems to have convinced himself that the physical manifestations, alleged to have taken place during the previous two months, were unquestionably authentic. Among other things he was informed that on 15 September, Mr Dagg had brought home a five-dollar bill and a two-dollar bill and gave them to his wife, who placed them in a bureau drawer. In the morning a little boy named Dean, an orphan, who was employed by various farmers as "chore boy", and who was temporarily in the service of the Daggs, came down from his bed in the garret and proceeded to light a fire in the cooking stove. Seeing on the floor a five-dollar bill he took it at once to Mr Dagg telling him where he had found it. Mr Dagg, being suspicious, looked in the drawer and discovered that the two-dollar bill was also gone. So sending the boy out of doors to milk, he examined his room and found his missing bill in his bed. Although convinced that the boy was guilty, they said nothing until later in the day when, on returning from the milk house, Mrs Dagg found on the floor of her house from back to front a streak of filth. This, with the theft of the money, was too much for Mrs Dagg and she immediately ordered the boy Dean out of the house. The boy stoutly asserted his innocence, but had to go. Mr Dagg took the boy to Shawville before a magistrate, and while they were away the same thing hap-

During the presidency of Abraham Lincoln the vogue for the new Spiritualism was at its height among fashionable people. Even the President – a far from fashionable man – was drawn into it. Colonel Simon F. Kase, a lobbyist who had several times met Lincoln to discuss a railroad project with him, tells of encountering the President at a seance in the home of Mrs Laurie and daughter Mrs Miller. She was known for making a piano beat time on the floor as she played while in trance.

Kase said of the occasion that Mrs Miller began to play, and the front of the piano in truth rose off the floor and beat the time of the tune with heavy thuds. Kase asked if he could sit on the instrument so that he could "verify to the world that it moved". The medium composedly answered that he and as many others as wished could sit on the piano. Four men did: Kase, a judge, and two of the soldiers who were accompanying Lincoln. Mrs Miller again began to play and the piano – heedless of its load – began to rise and thump, lifting at least four inches off the floor. Kase concluded ruefully: "It was too rough riding; we got off while the instrument beat the time until the tune was played out."

pened again and filth was found in various places, in the eatables, in the beds, etc., showing conclusively that the boy was in no way connected with it. This continued for about a week and was accompanied by various other antics. Milk-pans were emptied, butter was taken from the crocks and put into the pans. As a precaution the milk and eatables were then conveyed to the attic for safety, but just the same annoyances occurred there as had happened before. This attic had no doors or windows and no entrance except by a stair which led up to it from the kitchen, and no one could enter the place without being seen, as these things were done in the daytime. The worry about eatables was succeeded by the smashing of windows, the outbreak of fires, the pouring of water and much other mischief. One afternoon little Dinah felt her hair, which hung in a long braid down her back, suddenly pulled, and on her crying out, the family found her braid almost cut off. It had to be completely severed. Incidents of this kind recurred during two months, and then a new type of manifestation developed. A gruff voice, which at first was heard by Dinah alone, began to be audible to all who were present.

It was evening in Benares, India. The legendary Madame Blavatsky – the small dumpy Russian mystic and medium with a strangely magnetic personality – was surrounded by several Indian scholars, a German professor of Sanskrit, and her devoted disciple Colonel Olcott.

The professor observed with regret that the Indian sages of old were supposed to have been able to perform amazing feats, such as making roses fall from the sky, but that people said the days of such powers were over. Madame Blavatsky stared at him thoughtfully. "Oh, they say that, do they?" she demanded. "They say no one can do it now? Well, I'll show them; and you may tell them from me that if the modern Hindus were less sycophantic to their Western masters, less in love with their vices, and more like their ancestors in many ways, they would not have to make such a humiliating confession, nor get an old Western hippopotamus of a woman to prove the truth of their Shastras!"

She set her lips together firmly, and made a grand imperious sweep of her right hand. With a swish, exactly one dozen roses came cascading down.

Madame Blavatsky returned calmly to her conversation.

On the Saturday morning of Mr Woodcock's visit, he tried to have a private talk with Dinah and took the child to an open shed at the back of the house where she declared she had seen something. Dinah said: "Are you there, Mister?" To Mr Woodcock's intense astonishment, "a deep, gruff voice, as of an old man, seemingly within four or five feet from him, instantly replied in language which cannot be repeated here." The visitor, recovering from his astonishment, said: "Who are you?" To which the reply came: "I am the devil. I'll have you in my clutches. Get out of this or I'll break your neck."

From these beginnings a conversational wrangle developed which went on, we are told, for several hours. The voice used foul and obscene language, but in deference to the remonstrances of Mr Woodcock and George Dagg, after a while showed more restraint. The account insists that the gruff voice could not have been that of the child, which was rather exceptionally high-pitched, and also that there was no possible place of concealment where a practical joker could have hidden himself. As Mr Woodcock had heard of writings having been found about the house, he challenged the spirit to write something. Putting a sheet of paper and a pencil on a bench in the shed he saw the pencil stand up and move along the surface. As soon as the pencil dropped, he stepped over, and examining the paper said: "I asked you to write something decent." To this the voice replied in an angry tone, "I'll steal your pencil," and immediately the pencil rose from the bench and was thrown violently across the shed.

In the report given of the dialogue between the voice and its questioners, we find passages like the following:

Mr Dagg: "Why have you been bothering me and my family?"
Answer: "Just for fun."
Mr Dagg: "It was not very much fun when you threw a stone and struck little Mary."
Answer: "Poor wee Mary! I did not mean to hit her, I intended it for Dinah; but I did not let it hurt her."
Mr Dagg: "If it was only for fun why did you try to set the house on fire?"
Answer: "I didn't. The fires came always in the daytime and where you could see them. I'm sorry I did it."

In the end a promise was obtained from the spook that it would say good-bye and leave the house for good on the following night, the Sunday.

News of this spread, and there was great excitement throughout the neighbourhood. People began arriving early in the morning, and all the afternoon the place was thronged. The voice was on its good behaviour, as had been promised, but it answered questions and made comments on different people as they entered the room. Some remarks were very amusing and displayed an intimate knowledge of the private affairs of many of the questioners. One of the visitors commented on the change for the better in the language used. The reply thereupon came: "I am not the person who used the filthy language. I am an angel from Heaven sent by God to drive away that fellow." This character was maintained for some time, but Mr Woodcock declares that the voice was the same as that which they had previously heard, and, as the day wore on and many questions were asked, the spook contradicted himself, and getting entangled, lost his temper, saying many things quite out of harmony with his supposed heavenly origin.

Before ending his visit on the Sunday, Mr Woodcock drew up the following report:

To whom it may concern: We the undersigned solemnly declare that the following curious proceedings which began on the 15th day of September, 1889, and are still going on on the 17th day of November, 1889, in the house of Mr George Dagg, a farmer living seven miles from Shawville, Clarendon Township, Pontiac County, Province of Quebec, actually occurred as below described.

1st. That fires have broken out spontaneously throughout the house, as many as eight occurring in one day, six being in the house and two outside; that the window curtains were burned whilst on the windows, this happening in broad daylight, whilst the family and neighbours were in the house.

2nd. That stones were thrown by invisible hands through the windows, as many as eight panes of glass being broken, that articles such as a water jug, milk pitchers, a wash basin, cream tub, butter tub and other articles were thrown about the house by the same invisible agency, a jar of water being thrown in the face of Mrs John Dagg, also in the face of Mrs George Dagg while they were being about their household duties, Mrs George Dagg being alone in the house at the time it was thrown in her face; that a large dining table was thrown down; a mouth organ, which was lying on a small shelf, was distinctly heard to be played and was seen to move across the room on to the floor, while immediately after, a rocking chair began rocking furiously; that a washboard was sent flying down the stairs from the garret, no one being in the garret at the time. Further, that when the child Dinah is present a deep, gruff voice, like that of an aged man, has been heard at various times, both in the house and out of doors, and when asked questions has answered so as to be distinctly heard, showing that he is cognizant of all that has taken place, not only in Mr Dagg's family, but also in the families in the surrounding neighbourhood; that he claims to be a disincarnated being who died twenty years ago, aged about eighty years; that he gave his name to Mr George Dagg and Mr Willie Dagg, forbidding

> them to tell it; that this intelligence is able to make himself visible to Dinah, little Mary and Johnny, who have seen him under different forms at different times, at one time as a tall, thin man with a cow's head, horns, tail and a cloven foot, at another time as a big black dog, and finally as a man with a beautiful face and long white hair dressed in white, wearing a crown with stars in it.

This document is signed by seventeen witnesses, beginning with the Daggs, all of them responsible people living in the district. No women's names are included, and Mr Woodcock declares that he might have had twice as many signatures had he wanted them.

Perhaps the most extraordinary feature of the story is the fact that the spook after all took his departure in a blaze of glory. Though Mr Woodcock left the house on the Sunday evening to return to his own lodging, a number of people seem to have remained behind with the Daggs, hoping to witness the promised leavetaking of the author of all the disturbance. By this time he had, so far as appearances went, completely changed his character. He suddenly laid aside his gruff tones, declared that he had only maintained this harsh accent because otherwise people would have believed that Dinah was doing it, and then proceeded to sing hymns in what is described as a very beautiful flute-like voice. The group of visitors present were enchanted, and completely convinced by this reassumption of angelic attributes. So far from hastening the departure of the spook, they pressed him to stay, and this strange seance was prolonged until 3 am. The spirit then said goodbye, but promised to show himself to the children later in the morning.

Early in the forenoon of the Monday Mr Woodcock himself came back to the Dagg's house to take leave. He describes how, as he got there, "the three children, who had been out in the yard, came rushing into the house, wild-eyed and fearfully excited." I can only copy the exact terms of the statement which follows:

"Little Mary cried out 'Oh, Mama! the beautiful man! He took little Johnny and me in his arms, and, Oh, Mama, I played on the music and he went to Heaven and was all red!" They, the Daggs, rushed to the door, but nothing unusual was to be seen. On questioning the girls they both told the same story. Their accounts said it was a beautiful man, dressed in white, with ribbons and pretty things all over his clothes, with a lovely gold thing on his head and stars in it. They said he had a lovely face and long white hair, that he stooped down and took little Mary and the baby [Johnny] and said Johnny was a fine little fellow, and that Mary played on the music-thing he had with him. Dinah said she distinctly saw him stoop and lift Mary and Johnny in his arms and heard him speak to Johnny. Dinah said he spoke to her also and said – that man Woodcock thought he was not an angel, but he would show that he was, and then, she said, he went up to Heaven. On being questioned, she said he seemed to go right up in the air and disappear. He was in a kind of fire and the fire seemed to blaze up from his feet and surrounded him until he disappeared. No amount of questioning could shake their stories in the least."

What makes this case so interesting is that the poltergeist first declared itself to be the Devil, then an angel. It was obviously neither. We can also see that if the case had occurred a few centuries earlier, no one would have had the slightest doubt that they were dealing with real devils and angels. Is it possible that some of the stories about the devils and angels who appeared to saints in the Middle Ages were really about poltergeists up to their usual mischief?

The Esther Cox Case

But perhaps the most famous American haunting of the nineteenth century is the one that took place in Amherst, Nova Scotia, in 1878, and became known as "The Amherst Mystery".

A shoe worker, Daniel Teed, lived in a two-storey house with his wife and two sons, his wife's two unmarried sisters, Jane and Esther Cox, who were aged twenty-two and eighteen, his wife's brother William, and his own brother, John. (The house must have been grossly overcrowded.) All were Methodists. Jane, the elder sister, was pretty; Esther was short and rather stout. Nevertheless, Esther had a boyfriend, a local factory worker named Bob MacNeal.

In late August, Daniel Teed complained that someone had

been milking the cow; Esther was a suspect as she was unusually fond of milk. Esther was suffering from nervous tensions, and ran up from the cellar one night screaming that a rat had run over her leg. Her troubles were probably sexual in origin, as seems to be revealed by a dream she had at the time: hundreds of black bulls with bright blue eyes and blood dripping from their mouths tried to break into the house, while Esther frantically locked the doors . . .

The following evening, Esther and Bob MacNeal went out for a drive. Bob, who had a bad reputation locally, tried to persuade Esther to go into the woods with him, but she refused. He pulled out a gun and ordered her to get down from the buggy; he looked as if he might fire when the sound of an approaching vehicle distracted him. He leapt on to the buggy, drove back at a dangerous speed, let Esther off, then left Amherst for good. Esther cried herself to sleep, and for the next few days had red eyes.

On 4 September, a damp, misty evening, Jane heard Esther sobbing in bed. Then Esther screamed that there was a mouse in bed with her. They searched, but no mouse was found. The following night, both heard a rustling noise, and made a search. It seemed to be coming from a cardboard box containing patchwork, so Jane stood it in the middle of the room, expecting a mouse to run out. Instead the box jumped into the air and fell over. She stood it up, and it jumped again.

Daniel Teed came in to see what the noise was about, pushed the box under the bed, and told them to go to sleep.

The next night, Esther went to bed early. Soon after the light went out, she leapt out of bed shouting: "Jane, I'm dying." Jane lit the lamp and saw that Esther's face was bright red, and her hair was standing on end. Daniel Teed came in, together with the other two men. Esther got back into bed, but began to scream. Her body appeared to be swelling like a balloon. Suddenly, there was a loud report like a clap of thunder. The men rushed out to search the house, but found nothing. When they came back, Esther was back to normal and fast asleep.

Two days later, as Esther was getting into bed, she began to feel ill again. All the bedclothes flew off the bed, and landed in the far corner of the room. Jane fainted. Esther began to swell again. The men rushed in, and someone replaced the bedclothes; they promptly flew off again, and a pillow hit John Teed on the head; he left the house never to return. Again, there were some loud explosions. Esther stopped swelling, and fell asleep.

The following day, a doctor came to see Esther. As she lay in bed, the pillow under her head inflated, as if filled up with air, then collapsed, then re-inflated itself. Raps sounded around the room. The bedclothes flew off. There was a scratching noise above Esther's bed and, as they all watched, they saw writing appearing on the wall. It said: "Esther, you are mine to kill." A lump of plaster detached itself from elsewhere on the wall and flew across the room to the doctor's feet. Then rappings and bangs continued for the next two hours, while Esther lay, terrified, on her bed.

The following day, Esther complained of an "electric" feeling running through her body. The doctor gave her morphine; instantly, there was a series of bangs and crashes that seemed to go up to the roof.

These disturbances continued for another three weeks. Then, one night, Esther fell into a trance, became rigid, and told the story of what had happened with Bob MacNeal. When she recovered consciousness, she admitted it was true. When Jane said that Bob must be responsible for Esther's problems, loud knocks suggested that the "spirit" agreed completely. Jane remarked that it seemed to understand what she said, whereupon there were three distinct raps. The doctor tried asking the "spirit" simple questions, with one rap for no, two for "no answer", three for yes. But the doctor's attempts to get it to explain itself were a total failure.

Esther became a subject of controversy; the house was permanently full of people. When a minister called to see her, a bucket of cold water on the kitchen table began to bubble as if it was boiling.

In December, Esther developed a severe sore throat which turned to diphtheria. While she was ill, the manifestations ceased. Then she went away to convalesce. When she returned, the manifestations started immediately. Esther said she heard a voice telling her that the house was going to be set on fire. As she told the others about this, a lighted match fell from the air on to the bed, and the sheets caught fire. Jane quickly put it out. More lighted matches fell around the room, most of them going out immediately. The rapping noises started later, and when the family asked the "spirit" whether the house would be set alight, it replied that it would not be. At that moment there was smoke from under Esther's bed; they found that a dress had somehow transferred itself from the bedroom door, and had been set on fire.

Three days later, Mrs Teed smelled smoke coming from the cellar. They found a barrel of wood shavings burning vigorously and had some trouble putting it out.

The villagers were alarmed about this; if the Teed's house caught fire, half the village would probably be burned down. They suggested that Esther ought to be sent away. A neighbour named John White offered to take her in if she would do some housework. For two weeks, all went well; then a scrubbing brush flew out of Esther's hand, went up to the ceiling, and came down and hit her on the head.

White owned a restaurant, and Esther went to work there. An oven door refused to stay closed, and jumped off its hinges. Metal objects began flying at Esther as if she were a magnet, and a boy's clasp knife made her back bleed. When iron spikes were laid in her lap, they quickly became too hot to touch.

All this seemed to support the suspicion that Esther was somehow "electrified". They tried making her wear a special pair of shoes with glass soles; but these gave her headaches and made her nose bleed.

When furniture began to move around the restaurant, John White decided it was time for Esther to go home. Again, she left Amherst for a few months; first to stay with a man and his wife in New Brunswick, then to a farm three miles from Amherst. She told various visitors about the "voices" that spoke to her – voices which claimed to be the spirits that were causing the mischief. One of these spirits, "Bob Nickle", threatened her with fire and stabbing.

In June 1879, a stage magician named Walter Hubbell moved into the Teed's cottage as a paying guest; he had heard about the "haunting" and thought it might make the subject of a book. Within a few minutes of arriving, he had no doubt that this was no fraud. His umbrella sailed through the air, then a carving knife landed at his feet, then his bag was "thrown", then a chair shot across the room and hit his own so hard that he nearly fell on the floor. From then on, the chairs in every room he entered performed a dance. Esther told him he was unpopular with the spirits. Undeterred, Hubbell tried asking them questions by means of raps, and the spirits were able to tell him the number engraved on his watch, and the dates of coins in his pockets. Later, Hubbell lay down on the settee and closed his eyes; Esther came into the room, and Hubbell cautiously peeped at her, perhaps hoping that she would give herself away as a cheat. Instead, he saw a large glass paper-weight float up across the room and rebound off the arm of the settee.

During the next few days the poltergeist put on a special show for Hubbell. Objects floated around, strange noises were heard – like sawing wood and drumming on a washboard – and Esther was attacked by "six spirits" who stuck no fewer than thirty pins in her. Small fires broke out – on one day there were forty-five of them – and the sound of a trumpet echoed through the house; they later found a small silver trumpet which no one had ever seen before. When Esther went to the local minister to pray, "Bob Nickle" attacked her viciously on her return, cutting her head open with a bone and stabbing her in the face with a fork.

Hubbell thought he saw a way of making money. He hired a hall and persuaded Esther to put on a "show" for the people of Amherst. Inevitably, the spirits declined to operate, and the audience demanded their money back.

Tired of the non-stop disturbances, Daniel Teed sent Esther off to stay with some obliging friends; Hubbell, who now had enough material for his book, went to St John to write it. It appeared in due course and went through several editions.

During Esther's stay with her friends, the spirits let her alone. She then took a job on a farm owned by people called Davidson. Her friends found that various articles were missing, and these were located in the Davidsons' barn. Esther was suspected of theft, but before the case could be investigated the barn caught fire and burned to the ground. Esther was accused of arson, and was sentenced to four months in jail. After this, the manifestations came suddenly to an end.

This abrupt termination of the "haunting" seems to favour the view that Esther's own unconscious mind was responsible. This is, in fact, the view I favoured when I described the case briefly in a book called *Mysteries*. Esther was sexually frustrated, and if Bob MacNeal had adopted a more gentlemanly way of seducing her, there would have been no "Great Amherst Mystery" (the title of Hubbell's book). Esther was a classic case of "the divided self": a part of her longing to give herself to her lover, while the inhibitions induced by her background and training made this impossible. So when she rejected his advances, and he vanished into the night, her unconscious mind said, in effect, "Now see what you've done, stupid!", and set out to punish her. As to the effects themselves, many of them fit the hypothesis I have suggested: that the "energy" comes from the earth. When Esther wore shoes with glass soles, the manifestations stopped but she developed headaches and nosebleeds. Her sensation of electric currents is also highly suggestive. There have been dozens of well-authenticated cases of "human electric batteries". Again, nearly all concern girls or boys at the age of puberty. Caroline Clare of Bondon, Ontario, began to lose weight at the age of seventeen (in 1877), then developed such powerful electric currents that people who touched her received severe shocks; pieces of metal stuck to her as if she were a magnet. Jennie Morgan of Sedalia, Missouri, became an electric battery at fourteen; when she touched metal objects, sparks flew. Frank McKinistry, also of Missouri, would develop an electric charge during the night and slowly lose it during the day. When highly charged, his feet would stick to the ground so that he had difficulty in walking – which sounds again as if the electricity comes from the earth. (Good dowsers receive a "tingling" sensation when they touch standing stones.) The Amherst minister, the Reverend Edwin Clay, was convinced that the secret of Esther's manifestations was electricity, and even delivered a lecture to that effect.

But how did Esther's unconscious mind know the number of Hubbell's watch and the dates of coins in his pocket – which no doubt he did not know himself? How did her mind scratch "Esther, you are mine to kill" on the wall above her head? How did it blow a trumpet all over the house? The truth is that the unconscious mind theory needs to be stretched so much that it loses the chief virtue of a good theory – simplicity.

But perhaps the strongest argument against the unconscious mind theory is simply that Esther's torment went on for so long. To actually read the case in detail is to feel that no one could get so angry with herself that she would continue relentlessly for more than a year. We may say, "Oh, I could kick myself," when we do something stupid; but no one has ever *done* it.

The fraud hypothesis also fails to stand up to close examination. If Hubbell's book was the main piece of evidence, then we might well feel suspicious, since he went to Amherst with the hope of writing it, and eventually made a great deal of money from no fewer than ten editions. But there are accounts in the *Amherst Gazette* that confirm everything Hubbell says. Moreover, in 1907, more than a quarter of a century after the events, the researcher Hereward Carrington went to Amherst and took various depositions from people who had witnessed the manifestations. By this time, Esther was unhappily married, and had turned into a sullen middle-aged woman, who agreed to talk to Carrington only on the payment of a hundred dollars; Carrington felt that such testimony would be valueless. But there could be no doubt that most of the people involved believed that the manifestations were genuine, including the farmer, Davidson, whose barn had been destroyed – he said that he had often watched Esther as she came downstairs and had noticed that she seemed to fly or float.

In the Middle Ages, levitation used to be one of the signs of possession by demons – another interesting piece of evidence for the suggestion that demons were really poltergeists.

• chapter eight •

THE HAUNTING OF GLAMIS

Glamis Castle, in Angus, Scotland, has a reputation as one of the most haunted houses in the country. The oldest castle in Scotland, it will be remembered by readers of Shakespeare as the place where Macbeth murdered Duncan. Many of the legends associated with it are too silly to be taken seriously – such as the room in the tower where two earls are doomed to play dice forever as a punishment for cursing God, and the secret room that housed the famous Glamis Monster, a horrible misshapen creature like a large soft egg, born to one of the Lady Strathmores around 1800, and confined there in secrecy for the rest of his life. But too many people have seen the little Grey Lady who haunts the chapel for this to be dismissed as fiction. No one knows who she is, but several members of the Strathmore family have seen her, often kneeling in one of the pews. Glamis also seems to have a poltergeist which causes a loud crash in the old wing at four in the morning.

Lord Halifax, whose *Ghost Book* has become a classic of its kind, wrote a chapter on Glamis, where he often stayed. His name was Charles Wood, and he was born in 1839. His grandfather had been Prime Minister of England, but Charles Wood was more interested in religion than politics, and spent most of his life working for a union of the Catholic Church and the Church of England. Although an avid collector of ghost stories, he never joined the Society for Psychical Research, and it must be admitted that this shows in his famous *Ghost Book*, in which obviously factual stories are mixed up with absurd tales involving the devil and other sinister entities.

But at least he was familiar with Glamis, of which his brother in law was the owner until his sudden death in 1865. So much of his chapter on "The Secret of Glamis" is first hand reporting.

> In 1870 we met Miss Virginia Gabriel, fresh from a long visit to Glamis and full of the mysteries which had assumed such prominence since the death of our poor brother-in-law in 1865. The Chapel had been cleaned and re-dedicated with great solemnity, and the gossip was that the ghosts were endeavouring to terrify Claude (Lord Strathmore) and his family from making the Castle their home.
>
> I will try to write down all that Virginia told us, much of which was afterwards confirmed by Lady Strathmore. It appears that after my brother-in-law's funeral the lawyer and the agent initiated Claude into the family secret. He went from them to his wife and said: "My dearest, you know how often we have joked over the secret room and the family mystery. I have been into the room; I have heard the secret; and if you wish to please me you will *never* mention the subject to me again."
>
> Lady Strathmore was too good a wife not to obey, but she talked freely to other people, and her mother, old Mrs Oswald Smith, was one of the chief propagators of stories which, of course, lost nothing in the telling.
>
> Claude made a good many alterations and improvements at the Castle, one being a staircase from the lower hall or crypt, as it was called, to the Chapel, which had previously been accessible only through the great drawing-room. One day, when the family were in London, a man working in, I think, the Chapel, came upon a door opening up a long passage. He went some way down it; then became alarmed and went back and told the Clerk of the Works. Immediately all the work was stopped and the head man telegraphed to Claude in London and to Mr Dundas, the lawyer, in Edinburgh. Both arrived by the earliest possible train and subjected the workman to a severe examination as to what he

had or had not seen, the end of it being that he and his family were subsidized and induced to emigrate.

It is unquestionable that for many years, after the revelation of the secret, Claude was quite a changed man, silent and moody, with an anxious scared look on his face. So evident was the effect on him that his son, Glamis, when he came of age in 1876, absolutely refused to be enlightened.

Virginia further informed me that in several of the bedroom cupboards there were stones with rings in them. Claude converted all these cupboards into coal-stores, with strongly boarded fronts, and ordered them to be kept always full, so that no inquisitive visitor might attempt an exploration. She told us a wonderful tale of the first house-warming – a dance in the new dining-room in November 1869. They had all been very merry and dancing went on until the small hours. The three sets of rooms on the Clock Landing were occupied by the Streatfields (Lady Strathmore's sister), Mr and Lady F. Trevanion (Lord Strathmore's sister), and Mr and Mrs Monro from Lindertis. The latter were in the Red Room, their little boy sleeping in the dressing-room, the outer door of which was rather stiff and difficult to open. In the middle of the night, Mrs Monro awoke with a sensation as though someone was bending over her; indeed, I have heard that she felt a beard brush her face. The night-light having gone out, she called her husband to get up and find the matches. In the pale glimmer of the winter moon she saw a figure pass into the dressing-room. Creeping to the end of the bed she felt for and found the matchbox and struck a light, calling out loudly "Cam, Cam, I've found the matches."

To her surprise she saw that he had not moved from her side. Very sleepily he grumbled, "What are you bothering about?"

At that moment they heard a shriek of terror from the child in the dressing-room. Rushing in, they found him in great alarm, declaring that he had seen a giant. They took him into their own room, and while they were quieting him off to sleep they heard a fearful crash as though a heavy piece of furniture had fallen. At that moment the big clock struck four.

Nothing more happened, and the next morning Mr Monro extracted a reluctant promise from his wife to say nothing about her fright, as the subject was known to be distasteful to their host. However, when breakfast was half over, Fanny Trevanion came down, yawning and rubbing her eyes and complaining of a disturbed night. She always slept with a night-light and had her little dog with her on her bed. The dog, she said, had awakened her by howling. The night-light had gone out, and while she and her husband were hunting for matches they heard a tremendous crash, followed by the clock striking four. They were so frightened they could not sleep again.

Of course this was too much for Mrs Monro, who burst out with her story. No explanation was offered and the three couples agreed on the following night to watch in their respective rooms. Nothing was seen, but they all heard the same loud crash and rushed out on to the landing. As they stood there with scared faces the clock again struck four. That was all; and the noise was not heard again.

We did not go to Glamis that year, but with our heads full of all these wonderful tales paid a visit to Tullyallan Castle, a large and comfortable modern house. It was inhabited by a most cheerful old couple, Lord and Lady William Osborne, and there was nothing about it to suggest a ghost. On the night of the 28th of September I dreamt I was sleeping in the Blue Room at Glamis, which Addy and I occupied during our memorable and delightful visit in 1862. The dressing-room has a well-known trapdoor and a secret staircase leading to a corner of the drawing-room. I dreamt that I was in the park watching some horses when I heard the gong sound for dinner and rushed upstairs in a great hurry, begging the others not to wait for me. In the passage I met the housemaid coming out of the Blue dressing-room with her arms full of rusty bits of iron which she held out to me.

"Where did you find those?" I asked.

She replied that in cleaning the grate she had seen a stone with a ring in it which she had raised and in the hollow space below had found these pieces of iron.

I said, "I will take them down with me. His lordship likes to see everything that is found in the Castle."

As I opened the door of the Blue Room the thought crossed my mind: "They say the ghost always appears if anything is found. I wonder if he will come to me." I went in and there, seated in the armchair by the fire, I saw a huge figure of a man with a very long beard and an enormous stomach, which rose and fell with his breathing. I shook all over with terror, but walked to the fireplace and sat down on the coalbox staring at the ghost. Although he was breathing heavily I saw clearly that it was the face of a dead man.

The silence was unendurable, and at last I held up the pieces of rusty iron, saying, "Look what I have found" – an untruth, for the housemaid was the finder.

Then the ghost, heaving a deep sigh, said, "Yes, you have lifted a great weight off me. Those irons have been weighing me down ever since . . ."

"Ever since when?" I asked eagerly, forgetting my alarm in my curiosity.

"Ever since 1486," replied the ghost.

At that moment, to my great relief, I heard a knock at my door.

"That is Caroline" (my maid) I thought, "coming to dress me. I wonder if she will see this dreadful creature."

"Come in," I called and woke up.

It was Caroline opening my shutters, and the sun was streaming cheerfully into the room. I sat up in bed and found that my nightgown was quite wet with perspiration. I came downstairs very full of my dream, and still more of the fact, as I believed, that although the room was in all other respects exactly like the one I thought I remembered so well, the fire place was in a different corner. So persuaded was I of this that when next year I saw the room at Glamis and found that my dream memory was right and my waking memory wrong, I could scarcely believe my eyes. I even brought upon myself some ridicule by asking Claude if the fireplace had been changed, which would be neither easy nor likely in a house of that age and with walls of that thickness.

This part of my dream greatly interested Dr Acland and other Oxford dons as a striking confirmation of the theory that the brain receives impressions which are always accurate when it is undisturbed by outside influences. I wrote my dream down, but told it to very few people.

A year or two afterwards Mrs Wingfield, a daughter of Lord Castletown's, met my brother Eric at a water party and began asking him about my dream. She had had an odd experience of her own which unfortunately I can only relate second-hand, as I have never had the opportunity of meeting her.

So far as I could make out she was staying at Glamis for the first time during the same week, if not on the very same day, that we went to Tullyallan. She was occupying the Blue Room, but had heard none of the stories about Earl Beardie and his crew of ghosts. She went to bed with the usual night-light, which was so bright that she read by it before going to sleep. During the night she awoke with the feeling that someone was in the room, and sitting up in bed she saw, seated in front of the fire, a huge old man with a long, flowing beard. He turned his head and gazed fixedly at her, and then she saw that although his beard rose and fell as he breathed the face was that of a dead man. She was not particularly alarmed, but unfortunately made no attempt to enter into conversation with her visitor. After a few minutes he faded away and she went to sleep again.

Next morning, when Mr Oswald Smith began to tell her some of the tales of the Castle, she said, "Let me tell you first what I saw last night."

Whether she saw or dreamt it the coincidence was curious. Nothing came either of her dream or of mine, but some years afterwards, when we were driving from Glamis to Cortachy, my mother asked me if I had ever told my dream to Lady Strathmore. I replied that I had not thought it worth telling, but she insisted on my relating to Lady Strathmore just what I have written here. When I came to the date, Lady Strathmore gave a start, and turning to Fanny Trevanion, said, "Oh, that is too odd."

I said, "Surely that isn't the right date? I thought it was fifteen hundred and something."

"No," she answered, "it was in 1486, nearly four hundred years ago."

Of course I may have heard the date at some time, but have no recollection of it.

After 1870 we went to Glamis every year, nearly always spending my mother's birthday there. St Michael was the patron saint of the Chapel, people pretending that when it was re-dedicated he had been chosen for the purpose of keeping away evil spirits. I generally had a most ghostly little room, King Malcolm's Chamber, but never slept there, for my mother was so afraid of waking in the night and felt so nervous when she was alone that at Glamis I always slept with her.

We never saw or heard anything, and eager believers in the ghosts affirmed that this was because we had Lyon blood and the ghosts never appeared to any of the family. My mother's grandmother, Lady Anne Simpson, who was a Lyon, tried hard to see something and I often found her in her room with her face pressed against the window pane, straining her eyes for a glimpse of the White Lady, a most harmless apparition, who is supposed to flit about the avenue. One year on our arrival we found the whole house in great excitement as the White Lady had been seen by Lady Strathmore, her nieces and Lady Glasgow, from different windows at the same moment. Their descriptions were exceedingly vague and incoherent.

One more tale, related to me by old Dr Nicholson, the Dean of Brechin, I must put down. He said that once, when he was staying at Glamis, he had gone to bed in the room halfway up the winding stair. The door was locked, but he saw a tall figure enter, draped in a long, dark coat, fastened at the throat with a clasp. Neither spoke and the figure disappeared in the wall.

The Bishop of Brechin, Dr Forbes, who was also staying in the Castle, was very incredulous about this apparition and teased his friend by saying, "Now, Mr Dean, we all know you are the most persevering beggar in Scotland. I am sure you brought out your collecting book and laid the ghost by asking him for a subscription."

Next night, to the delight of Dr Nicholson, the Provost of Perth, who had joined the party, said he had had a similar mysterious visit the last time he slept in that room. The Dean at once hurried him off to the Bishop and made him repeat his tale to that sceptical prelate.

Bishop Forbes and Uncle Robert Liddell both offered to hold a service of exorcism in the Castle, but this was never done. I think Claude would have been afraid to have it. Unquestionably, there is something strange about the place. The Chaplain told me that he felt this more and more the longer he lived there, while the Factor, Mr Ralston, a dry, shrewd, hard-headed Scotsman, after he had been initiated into the secret could never be induced to sleep in the Castle. One winter evening, when he had come up for the theatricals, a sudden snowstorm came on and the road back to his home appeared impassable. However, he resolutely refused to spend the night on a sofa and insisted on rousing the gardeners and stablemen to dig out a path to his house nearly a mile off outside the Park. Lady Strathmore herself told me that she once disclosed to Mr Ralston her great curiosity about the mystery. He looked earnestly at her and said very gravely: "Lady Strathmore, it is fortunate that you do not know it and can never know it, for if you did you would not be a happy woman." Such a speech from such a man was certainly uncanny.

Many years afterwards, in September 1912, I visited Glamis with my daughter, Dora, for the first time after Claude's death. His son, the present owner, has no objection to talking about the ghost.

He and his wife were much interested in my dream and got me to give them a copy of my account of it. Lady Strathmore told me that on her first visit to Glamis after her marriage she and her husband occupied the Blue Room. During the night she dreamt that she saw a big man gazing at her from the other side of the bed; only he was thin, not fat like my ghost. She woke in a great fright and roused her husband, but of course there was nothing there. Two of her children, Rose, the second girl, and David, the youngest boy, often see shadowy figures flitting about the Castle. They are not alarmed by them, but Rose says she would not like to sleep in the Blue Room. Figures have been frequently seen by them and by a housemaid in the Oak Room, which my mother always had, but it has now been turned into an extra sitting-room. King Malcolm's Chamber, the little room where I used to dress, has also been dismantled and thrown into the passage. This is a great improvement, as it provides a better access to the great drawing-room and the Chapel.

• chapter nine •

BORLEY RECTORY

The most famous haunted house in England is undoubtedly Borley Rectory. And the man who made it famous is England's most remarkable ghost-hunter, Harry Price.

Price, ghost-hunter extraordinary, claimed that he was born in Shrewsbury, son of a wealthy paper manufacturer. A brilliant critical biography by Trevor Hall, *The Search for Harry Price,* reveals that he was, in fact, the son of an unsuccessful grocer, and that he was born in London in 1881. From then until he was about forty he seems to have supported himself by a variety of jobs, including commercial travelling, manufacturing patent medicines, journalism and giving gramophone concerts. What *is* certain is that his lifelong interest in stage magic began at the age of eight, when he saw an itinerant magician and patent medicine salesman, the Great Sequah, giving a public performance. Price began collecting books on magic, and became an expert magician. It may have been the interest in magic that led him to join the Society for Psychical Research in 1920 – the SPR was then, as now, much concerned with trying to detect fraud in mediums. E.J. Dingwall, who was then Research Officer for the Society, asked Price if he would care to come with him to Munich, to attend some seances of a remarkable German medium, Willi Schneider – one of two brothers. The man who arranged the seances was the German investigator, Baron von Schrenk-Notzing, a friend of Lombroso's, and the author of a sensationally successful book called

Materialisation Phenomena, which had aroused widespread scepticism in Germany when it appeared in 1914. Schrenk-Notzing himself was something of a flamboyant publicist, and Trevor Hall suggests that Harry Price took his example to heart, and decided that this was the way to achieve the fame he craved. (He admitted frankly that he had always wanted to get his name in *Who's Who*.)

The Schneider brothers, Willi and Rudi, the most psychic members of a psychic family, were born at Braunau-am-Inn and, according to one friend of the family, the phenomena began after they had spent an evening playing with a ouija board. Willi had then reached the age of puberty – in 1916 – and the family was disturbed by loud knocking noises. Then objects began moving around, and Willi saw a ghost in the sitting room. Neighbours became so alarmed about the racket that the family were on the point of vacating the flat. By means of the ouija board, they tried questioning the "spirit", which identified itself as a girl named Olga Lindtner, who claimed to be a reincarnation of the notorious Lola Montez. In due course, Willi went into a trance, and Olga spoke through him. In spite of doubts later raised by Harry Price – after he had quarrelled with the brothers – there can be no doubt that the phenomena were genuine. The novelist Thomas Mann attended one seance, and has recorded how, as he pressed Willi's knees tightly between his own, and two other people held his hands, a handkerchief floated into the air, a bell began to ring and then floated into the air, a music box played, and the keys of a typewriter were struck. Mann was convinced that deception was impossible.

Harry Price and E.J. Dingwall witnessed similar occurrences, and also saw a white hand which materialised in front of them; they had no doubt whatever of the genuineness of the phenomena, and said as much at a lecture to the SPR. But by way of keeping his options open, Price helped to edit and publish a book called *Revelations of a Spirit Medium,* in which a fake medium described the tricks of the trade.

The case with which Price's name has become most widely associated is, of course, that of Borley Rectory. And in spite of the debunking that has taken place since Price's death in 1948, it remains one of the most interesting hauntings of the twentieth century. After Price's death, a whole volume of the *Proceedings of the Society for Psychical Research* was devoted to *The Haunting of Borley Rectory,* "A Critical Survey of the Evidence", by

Dingwall, Trevor Hall and Kate Goldney. They allege that Price probably produced some of the "poltergeist" phenomena himself by tossing pebbles – which, from our knowledge of Price, must be admitted as possible. Their overall conclusion is that there are so many doubts that it would probably be simplest to regard the haunting of Borley as a fairy story. But this is to ignore the fact that stories of hauntings were common long before Price came on the scene, and have continued since he left it. Anyone who feels that the SPR survey proves that Price was a liar should read the long account of Borley in Peter Underwood's *Gazetteer of British Ghosts*, with Underwood's own firsthand reports from interviews with witnesses.

Borley Rectory was built in 1863 on the site of Borley Manor House, which in turn seems to have been built on the site of a Benedictine abbey. It was built by the Reverend H.D.E. Bull. It is difficult to pin down the earliest known "sightings", but it is clear that during Henry Bull's tenancy, a number of people saw the apparition of a nun. Henry Bull himself knew of the legend that a nun and a Benedictine monk had tried to elope, been caught, and had both been killed, the nun being bricked up alive. Bull's daughter Ethel confirmed in a letter to Trevor Hall in 1953 that she had awakened to find a strange man standing beside her bed, and had felt someone sitting down on the bed on several occasions; she also told Peter Underwood how, on 28 July 1900, she and her two sisters all saw a nun-like figure gliding along "Nun's Walk", apparently telling her beads. The other sister, Elsie, saw the nun, who looked quite solid, and went to ask her what she wanted; the nun vanished.

After the Reverend Henry Bull's death, his son, the Reverend Harry Bull, took over the rectory. He was interested in psychical research, and claimed that he saw many ghosts. His daughter told Price that he had seen a legendary phantom coach (in which the lovers were supposed to have fled) and that, one day in the garden, the retriever had howled with terror, looking towards some legs visible under a fruit tree. Bull, thinking this was a poacher, followed the legs as they walked towards a postern gate; at which point he realised that the "poacher" was somehow incomplete. The legs disappeared through the gate without opening it.

Harry Bull died in 1927, and the rectory was empty until 1928, when the Reverend Guy Smith and his wife moved in.

One stormy night, there was a furious ringing of the doorbell;

Borley Rectory

when Smith arrived there, he found no one. It happened again later – a peal so prolonged that Smith was able to get to the door before it stopped; again, there was no one. After that, all the keys of all the rooms fell out of the locks overnight; later, they vanished. Then they began hearing slippered footsteps. Stones were thrown – small pebbles. Lights were switched on. One day, Mrs Smith thought she saw a horse-drawn coach in the drive. Mr Smith thought he heard someone whisper, "Don't, Carlos, don't", as he was walking into the chapel. The Smiths decided to contact the *Daily Mirror*, who asked Harry Price if he would be willing to go along with an investigator. They told Price their story, and gave him every facility to investigate. But within nine months, they had had enough of the place – perhaps because its plumbing left much to be desired – and moved to Norfolk. According to the SPR report, the Smiths only called the *Daily Mirror* because they were concerned about all the stories that the house was haunted, and wanted to reassure their parishioners by getting the place a clean bill of health. This story sounds, on the face of it, absurd. Moreover, there exists a letter from Mr Smith to Harry Price stating: "Borley is undoubtedly haunted." (It is true that Mrs Smith wrote a letter to the *Church Times* in 1929 saying she did not believe the house to be haunted, but this seems to have been a belated attempt to stem the flood of sensational publicity that followed the *Daily Mirror* story.)

In October 1930, the rectory was taken over by the Reverend L.A. Foyster, and his much younger wife Marianne. Foyster, oddly enough, had lived near Amherst at the time of the Esther Cox case, and the SPR survey makes much of this coincidence; however, it seems doubtful that the vicar would attempt to fake disturbances on the model of his earlier experience. Certainly, the Foyster incumbency saw the most spectacular exhibitions of the Borley poltergeist. Foyster kept a diary of the disturbances. Bells were rung, bricks thrown, footsteps heard and water out of a jug poured over the couple when in bed. Foyster was even awakened by a violent blow on the head from his own hairbrush. They saw a number of apparitions, including the nun and a clergyman who was identified as the Reverend Henry Bull, the builder of the rectory. Writing appeared on the walls, asking for a mass to be said, and asking for "Light".

There is much independent confirmation of all these events. A Justice of the Peace named Guy L'Estrange visited Borley at the invitation of the Foysters, and wrote a lengthy account of it.

As soon as he arrived, he saw a dim figure near the porch, which vanished as soon as he approached. Mrs Foyster had a bruise on her forehead – something "like a man's fist" had struck her the previous evening. The Foysters were telling L'Estrange about mysterious fires that kept breaking out in locked rooms when there was a loud crash in the hall; they found it littered with broken crockery. Then bottles began flying about. L'Estrange notes that they seemed to appear suddenly in mid-air. The bottles were coming from a locked storage shed outside. All the bells began to ring, making a deafening clamour – but all the bell wires had been cut. L'Estrange shouted: "If some invisible person is present, please stop ringing for a moment." Instantly, the bells stopped – stopped dead, as if each clapper had been grabbed by an unseen hand. Later, sitting alone in front of the fire, L'Estrange heard footsteps behind him; he turned, but the room was empty. The footsteps had come from a part of the wall where there had once been a door. In bed, L'Estrange felt the room become icy cold, and saw a kind of shape materialising from a patch of luminosity; he walked towards it, and had a feeling of something trying to push him back. He spoke to it, and it slowly vanished. He was luckier than another visitor who thought that the ghostly figure was someone playing a joke, and tried to grab it; he was given a hard blow in the eye.

The rector and others tried praying in the chapel, taking with them a relic of the Curé of Ars, and then went around the house making signs of the cross. Finally, they all spent the night in the Blue Room, where Henry Bull (and others) had died; they asked that the entity should stop troubling the inmates of the house; a black shadow began to form against the wall, then dissolved. But after this, temporary peace descended on Borley Rectory.

In 1935, the Foysters decided they had had enough, and moved. Price rented the rectory in 1937, and arranged for a team of investigators to go in. But the major phenomena were over. Even so, the chief investigator, Sidney Glanville, a retired engineer, became completely convinced of the reality of the haunting.

In March 1938, the team were experimenting with a planchette, which wrote the message that Borley would be destroyed by fire. This happened in February 1939, when the house mysteriously burned down. Yet the phenomena continued; a Cambridge team investigating the ruins heard footsteps, saw patches of light, and recorded sudden sharp drops in temperature.

In August 1943, Price decided to try digging in the cellars at Borley – which he had been advised to do by a planchette message which claimed to come from "Glanvil" – the same Glanvil who wrote the account of the Tedworth drummer. They found a cream jug, which had also been referred to by the planchette, and some fragments of a human skull. The jawbone showed signs of a deep-seated abscess – Peter Underwood speculates that this is why the phantom nun always looked miserable.

The SPR survey on Borley, which appeared eight years after Price's death, had the effect of seriously undermining his credit. Trevor Hall's *Search for Harry Price* (1978) completed the work of destroying his reputation. Yet although this leaves no doubt that Price lied about his origins – perhaps romanced would be a better word – and hungered for fame, it produces no evidence that Price was not exactly what he always claimed to be: an enthusiastic scientific investigator of paranormal phenomena. To assume that, because Price wanted to be thought a "gentleman", he was also dishonest as a paranormal researcher, is surely poor psychology. Price was one of those ambitious men who crave an outlet for their energies. He was forty years old before he found the opportunity he was looking for – a long time for a man of Price's impatient temperament. It came when Dingwall invited him to Munich to study the Schneider brothers. From then on, Price had discovered his vocation; at last, he had found the outlet he needed for his explosive energy and romanticism. And when a man as energetic and romantic as Harry Price finally finds what he is looking for, he does not risk spoiling everything with a little cheap skulduggery. It only takes one scandal to destroy a scientist's reputation. But to put it this way is to imply that Price disciplined his natural dishonesty solely to maintain his reputation and this is to miss the real point; that once a man has found his vocation, he pours into it all that is best about himself. Bernard Shaw has left an interesting description of the socialist Edward Aveling, who was Eleanor Marx's common-law husband; he was an inveterate seducer, and a borrower who never paid his debts, yet where socialism was concerned, he was fiercely sincere. Everything we know about Price reveals that, where psychical research was concerned, he was totally dedicated – although not above grabbing publicity wherever he could find it.

Unlike most automatic writers, who received their messages from the spirits, the nineteenth century British journalist William Stead got messages from the living – and saved them the bother of writing themselves. He would ask mental questions and his hand would write the answers automatically – sometimes learning more than the friends wanted him to.

Once he had arranged a lunch engagement with a woman who had been out of town over the weekend. He mentally inquired whether she had returned to London yet, and his hand wrote a long note. It described an unpleasant encounter she had had on the train. According to the message, she had found herself alone in a compartment with a strange man. He came over, sat close to her, and when she tried to push him away, attempted to kiss her. Struggling furiously, she thumped him with his umbrella, which broke. Then the train unexpectedly stopped and the man took flight.

When Stead sent his servant to his friend's house with a note condoling her on the assault, the woman was taken aback. She replied, "I had decided not to speak of it to anyone." She added, "The umbrella was mine, not his."

In short it would be of no advantage to him to pretend the Borley phenomena were genuine when they were not. His reputation was based on his scepticism as much as on his support of the reality of psychic phenomena. Possibly – like most of us – he was capable of stretching a fact when it appealed to his romanticism. But in the case of Borley, there was no need to stretch facts. The haunting of Borley does not rest on Price's evidence alone; there are dozens of other witnesses, such as Guy L'Estrange – or Dom Richard Whitehouse, cited by Underwood, who witnessed just as many incredible occurrences: flying objects, ringing of bells, writing on walls, outbreaks of fire, materialisation of bottles.

And is there evidence that Price *did* stretch the facts? The SPR survey cites as an example of his dishonesty the episode of the pair of legs that Harry Bull saw walking through the postern gate. Price says, admittedly, that when the man emerged from behind the fruit trees, he was headless. But the report then goes on to cite Price's original notes, which read: "Rev. Harry Bull saw coach, Juvenal, retriever, terrified and growled. Saw man's legs rest hid by fruit trees, thought poacher, followed with

Juvenal, gate shut, but saw legs disappear through gate." Clearly, what Bull saw disappearing through the gate was not a complete man, or Price would not refer only to the legs. It sounds as if the upper half of his body was missing – in which case, headless is a fair description.

What seems clear from all accounts of the case is that the "ground" itself is haunted, and continues to be so. Borley is a "place of power", the kind of place that *would* be chosen for a monastery, and that probably held some pagan site of worship long before that. In the Rectory's early days, Harry Bull himself – son of the Reverend Henry Bull – was probably the unconscious focus or medium; Paul Tabori says that he was probably psychic. This is borne out by the fact that young Bull saw so many of the "ghosts", including the coach and the nun. It is important to realise that not all people can see ghosts. The "ghost-hunter" Andrew Green describes, in *Our Haunted Kingdom,* a visit that he and other members of the Ealing Psychical Research Society paid to Borley in 1951.

"One of the Society members grabbed my arm and, although

One night in early spring 1948, a young Swedish man awoke to find a white-haired gentleman standing at his bedside. For some reason the young man – whom we'll call Erson – wasn't frightened. The stranger began to talk in a language Erson couldn't understand, but thought must be English. He managed to convey the information that his name was Price.

The mysterious Price began to appear fairly frequently, at times in the morning, and he was seen not only by Erson but also by his wife and daughter. The figure appeared solid and lifelike, but when Erson tried to photograph it, he only got a few shadows on the prints. Price seemed amused by these efforts to photograph him.

Finally Erson acquired enough English to understand that his visitor had studied ghosts and related subjects when alive. It was "Price" who urged Erson to go to a particular hospital in Lund to take treatment for a health problem. While there, Erson told a psychiatrist of his ghostly visitor. The doctor, having heard of the famous English psychical researcher Harry Price, decided to find out from the SPR when he had died. It was 29 March 1948 – just about the time that Erson's spectral friend had made his first appearance.

obviously terrified, proceeded to describe a phantom that he could see some thirty feet in front of him, standing at the end of the 'Nun's Walk". It was of a Woman in a long white gown, and moved slowly towards the end of the neglected garden . . . the witness was perspiring profusely with fear and later with annoyance that I had failed to see the ghost."

Green had only *heard* the rustle of trees and bushes, as if something was walking through the undergrowth. We may assume, then, that if Green had been a tenant of Borley before its destruction, he would probably have seen no ghosts. Bull *was*, it seems, enough of a "medium" to see the ghosts. And Marianne Foyster was a far more powerful medium who changed the character of the haunting into poltergeist activity. (Most of the messages scrawled on walls were addressed to her.) The reason that the subsequent investigation of Borley (during Price's tenancy) was so unsuccessful was that there was no medium present to provide the energy.

Asked about the "ley system" of the Borley area, the ley expert Stephen Jenkins replied as follows: "Norfolk and Suffolk are a spider-web of alignments, many of which are linked to curious manifestations. Borley church stands at a node where four lines cross, one going from Asher church to Sproughton church . . ." After giving further details of the ley system, he goes on:

> My wife photographed me as I was standing with my back to the south wall of Borley churchyard, at ten o'clock on the morning of Saturday the 1st of September, 1979. Recently, this was borrowed for a magazine article, and the editor kindly sent me an enlargement. No less than three people, not one of them known to the others, have on separate occasions noted in the enlargement some odd – and not very prepossessing – faces among the trees close to the church. The same identifications have been made without possibility of collusion.
>
> More dramatic than unexpected faces in a photograph, which can always be explained away as "simulacra", or something wrong with the emulsion, is an incident of Sunday the 28th of August, 1977, on the road north of Belchamp Walter Hall. The time was precisely 12:52 pm, and we were driving south west along the minor road which marks the

north end of the Hall grounds, when on the road in front, in the act of turning left into the hedge (I mean our left, across the path of the car), *instantaneously* appeared four men in black – I thought them hooded and cloaked – carrying a black, old-fashioned coffin, ornately trimmed with silver. The impression made on both of us was one of absolute *physical* presence, of complete material reality. Thelma and I at once agreed to make separate notes without comparing impressions. We did so, and the descriptions tallied exactly, except that she noted the near left bearer turn his face towards her. I did not see this as I was abruptly braking at the time.

What I had seen as a hood, she described as a soft tall hat, with a kind of scarf falling to the left shoulder, thrown across the cloaked body to the right. The face was that of a skull.

The next day we returned to the precise spot at exactly the same time and took a picture. It is a Kodak colour slide. In the hedge near the gap where the "funeral party" vanished (there is a path there leading to Belchamp Walter churchyard) is a short figure, apparently cloaked, its face lowered with a skull-like dome to the head. A year later I returned searching the area where it had apparently stood. There was nothing, no post or stump that might have provided such an image, nor was there the slightest sign of the ground having been disturbed by the removal of anything that might have been rooted in it. The image is simply there on the film – we saw nothing wrong with the eye.

That minor road alongside the north edge of the Belchamp Walter Estate precisely coincides with a line passing through the node in the water west of Heaven Wood. That node itself linked with the node at Borley.

He adds a postscript: "I hazard a guess that the dress of the coffin-bearer is that of the late fourteenth century. There seems to be no local legend of a phantom funeral."

If Price invented the ghosts of Borley, he must have been in collusion with a remarkable number of people.

The English medium Rosemary Brown has produced quantities of music she claims has been dictated to her by the great masters of music, who have chosen this way to prove that their spirits survive. One of her special favourites is Beethoven, and the two of them are engaged on a project that is taking years: the Tenth Symphony. It is an enormous choral work, like the great composer's Ninth Symphony.

In writing this new work Beethoven will be able to hear it, according to Rosemary Brown. In her autobiography *Unfinished Symphonies*, she says that his deafness is gone. "Those human ills and frailties disappear once we reach the other side," she writes. The spirit Beethoven is a less stormy person than he was in life, but he is still awe-inspiring. Rosemary Brown was so much in awe of him at first that little conversation took place. She received his music by a kind of telepathy, slowly catching his ideas in writing.

Now Beethoven works much more directly, dictating several bars for one hand, and then going back to fill in for the other. "After all," says the medium, "they know already what they are going to tell me to write, and it is simpler to keep to one line at a time."